Spoilt Rotten

The Toxic Cult of Sentimentality

THEODORE DALRYMPLE

London

GIBSON SQUARE

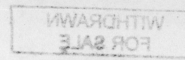

This edition first published in 2011 by Gibson Square

UK Tel: +44 (0)20 7096 1100
    Fax: +44 (0)20 7993 2214

US Tel: +1 646 216 9813
    Fax: +1 646 216 9488

Eire Tel: +353 (0)1 657 1057

    info@gibsonsquare.com
    www.gibsonsquare.com

    ISBN 9781906142254

Printed by CPI Mackay.

Contents

'Only a man with a heart of stone could read of the death
of Little Nell without laughing.'
Oscar Wilde

'I'll thcream and thcream and thcream until I'm thick
— I can you know.'
Violet Elizabeth, in Just William by Richmal Crompton

Introduction

Children

A recent report by the United Nations Children's and Educational Fund (UNICEF) stated that Britain was the worst country of twenty-one advanced countries in which to be a child. Normally I do not set much store by these kind of league-table statements, which are usually based upon many false premises, suppositions and the like, and are designed to produce the very results that will confirm their authors' prejudices (or their authors' employers' prejudices). Rarely do such reports fail to suggest that more government intervention in people's lives is the answer to the problems with which they deal.

But the UNICEF report is right, *grosso modo*. If there is a country in the developed world in which childhood is a more wretched experience than in Britain, I do not know it. It is wretched not only for those experiencing it themselves, but for those experiencing British children. The British are a nation that fears its own children.

I see this at the bus stop in the little town in Britain in which I live some of the year. By prevailing standards, the children of this town are by no means bad, but their mere presence in any numbers makes old people at the bus-stop shrivel into themselves, and huddle up together for protection, as the Voortrekkers in South Africa used to form a circle of their wagons at night when travelling through potentially hostile territory. If a child misbehaves — dropping litter, spitting, swearing loudly, bullying another child, pulling hair, drinking alcohol — the old people notice, but say nothing. Tempers these days are short, knives are often long, and children quickly band together to defend their inalienable right to utter egotism.

In Britain, violence committed by and on children has increased very rapidly. The emergency departments of out hospitals report a dramatic rise in such cases, fifty per cent in five years, involving tens of thousands of cases. Teachers are increasingly subjected to threats from their pupils. In the year 2005-6, for example, 87,610 children, that is to say 2.7 per cent of all children at secondary school, were excluded for a time because of verbal or physical attacks on teacher (in Manchester, 5.3 per cent of secondary pupils were so excluded, and it is an unfortunate fact that where metropolitan areas lead, other areas usually follow).

A recent survey showed that a third of British teachers

had suffered physical attacks from children, and a tenth of them had been injured by children. Nearly two thirds had been verbally abused and insulted by children. A half of them had thought of leaving the teaching profession because of the unruly behaviour of children, and as many knew of colleagues who had done so.

As if this were not bad enough, five-eighths as many teachers have faced aggression from parents as from the pupils themselves. That is to say, teachers cannot rely on parents to back them up in trying to deal with an unruly, aggressive or violent child, quite the contrary. (This is exactly what my patients who were teachers told me.)

The complacent suggest that 'twas ever thus, and in a sense they are right. There is no kind of human behaviour that is utterly without precedent: the world is too old for people to invent wholly new ways of behaving. For every act of viciousness, malignity or brutality, there is always an historical precedent. Nevertheless, it is within living memory that in most cases when a child misbehaved in school, and his parents were informed of it by a teacher, the child could expect retribution at home as well as discipline at school. Now, in a large number of cases, he can expect neither. The question is not whether each individual case is without precedent — clearly it is not — but whether the number of cases has increased, and whether there is any reason, other than a decline in the numbers of children, that it should decrease.

It is not only teachers who suffer from the aggression and violence of parents. An article published in 2000 in the *Archives of Diseases of Childhood* found that nine out of ten trainees in paediatric medicine in Britain had witnessed a violent incident involving a child, nearly half of them within the last year, four out of ten had been threatened by a parent, five per cent had actually been assaulted, and ten per cent had been the object of an attempted assault.

It is important to understand that these figures are quite enough to produce a permanent atmosphere of intimidation, and that this atmosphere of intimidation pervades everything. A single incident has a powerful demonstration effect. Here I will give two examples, drawn from slightly different spheres, of how behaviour is changed by such an atmosphere.

I once had a patient who claimed that he had not worked for a long time because he had a back injury. He received a certificate of ill-health and exemption from work from his general practitioner. Despite his back injury that allegedly prevented him from working, his main interests were judo and jogging, which he did every night without fail. I noticed that in the hospital he got on and off his bed without the slightest difficulty or suggestion of back pain. In short, he was an exceptionally fit and athletic young man.

I telephoned his general practitioner to inform him of my finding, suggesting that his alleged back injury could not justify a certificate of ill-health.

'Oh, I know all that,' said the general practitioner to me, as if I were being very naïve in supposing that a certificate should be based upon the truth. 'But the last time I refused to give such a certificate to someone, he picked up the computer on my desk and threw it at me, and before long we were rolling about on the floor. Since then I have given a sick certificate to anyone who wanted one.'

This, no doubt, helps to explain how it has come about that, despite ever-rising levels of health, as measured objectively, Britain now has millions of certified invalids, more indeed than after the First World War. A relatively small amount of violence is sufficient to produce a large effect.

The second example is that of forced marriage among young women born in Britain of Pakistani descent. Many of them were taken by their parents to Pakistan during their adolescence to be married to a first cousin in the village from which their parents had emigrated. I am no stranger to the varieties of human suffering, but the suffering of these young women to whom the prospect of such a marriage was repellent, and an abomination, was among the worst I have ever encountered.

All of these young women knew of cases in which someone in their situation had been horribly done to death by her own family because she had refused absolutely to go along with such a marriage, thereby dishonouring the family, whose word had been given. The situation of the eldest daughter was particularly acute, for her parents felt that as she went, so went the other members of the family.

Cases of honour-killing, so called, do not need to be very many for them to dissolve the distinction between voluntary and involuntary acceptance of marriage to a first cousin chosen by a young woman's parents. The very atmosphere that they create, though not numerous, make it difficult to investigate objectively their real frequency and effect.[1]

Once again, a small amount of violence is sufficient to have a large effect.

Let us now return to the question of childhood in Britain. Are there any intelligible reasons why children and their parents who, by the standards of all previous generations, some of them not so very long ago,[2] enjoy excellent conditions of physical health and access to undreamed of sources of knowledge and entertainment, should be anxiety-ridden, aggressive and violent?

There are, and many of them have their origin in sentimentality, the cult of feeling.

The Romantics emphasised the innocence and inherent goodness of children, compared with the moral degradation of adults. The way to make better adults, then, and to ensure that such degradation did not take place, was to find the right way of preserving their innocence and goodness. The right education became the prevention of education.

Along with their innocence and goodness went, or were ascribed to them, other attributes, like intelligent curiosity, natural talent, vivid imagination, desire to learn and ability to find out things for themselves. If the evidence that children were not equal in all respects was too strong to be absolutely denied, the fiction was substituted that all children were endowed with at least one special talent,[3] and in that way were equal — all talents being equal, of course.

Romantic educational theory, subsequently provided with a patina of science by committed researchers, is full of absurdities that would be delightfully laughable had they not been taken seriously and used as the basis of educational policy to impoverish millions of lives. Romanticism has penetrated into the very fibre of the educational system, affecting even the way in which children were taught to read. Despising routine and rote, and pretending that in all circumstances they were counterproductive or even deeply harmful, and much hated by children, the romantic educational theorists came up with the idea that children would learn to read better if they discovered how to do so for themselves. Thus, partly on the pretext that English is not a phonetic language (though it is not completely unphonetic either, and indeed the majority of its words are written phonetically), children were presented with whole words and sentences in the hope that they would eventually deduce the principles of spelling and grammar. This is only slightly more sensible than sitting a child under an apple in the hope that it will arrive at the theory of gravity. Most children need a clue, and even those few who don't could spend their time more profitably on other things. Here I shall give only a selection of some of the things that have been said, apparently believed and acted upon.[4]

In the examination of any intellectual or social trend, it is impossible to reach its sole and indisputable source, as it is possible to do for some rivers, nor is it necessary to do so. All that is necessary is to show that the trend exists and that it has its intellectual antecedents.

The theorists of education of the nineteenth century and first part of the twentieth laid the foundations for schools that, in large parts of the country, have become little more than elaborate baby-sitting services and the means by which children are kept off the streets, where they might act like piranha fish in a South American river. Never in the field of human history has so little been imparted to so many at such great expense. In Britain, we now spend four times as much per head on education as in 1950; but it is very doubtful whether the standard of literacy in the general population has increased, and it is far from impossible that it might have decreased.

In the area in which I worked, a poor one, I discovered that the majority of my patients who had recently emerged from eleven years of compulsory education, or at any rate of compulsory attendance at school, could not read a simple text with facility. They would stumble over longer words, and would often be completely unable to decipher words of three syllables, pointing to an offending word and saying, 'I don't know that one', as if English were written in ideograms rather than alphabetically. When asked to put into their own words what the passage meant that they had just stumbled through, they would say 'I don't know, I was only reading it.' When asked whether they were any good at arithmetic, half of them replied 'What's arithmetic?' As to their arithmetical ability itself, it can perhaps best be grasped by the reply that one eighteen year-old gave me to the question 'What is three times four?'

'I don't know,' he said, 'we didn't get that far.'

I should point out that these young people were not of deficient intelligence, and in any case I discovered that the mentally-handicapped children of middle class professional parents, who had taken care to educate those children to the maximum of their capacity, were often better able to read and reckon than their much more intelligent age-peers from working-class, or sub-working-class, backgrounds.

Nor was the virtual illiteracy of the young people compensated for by any great development of memory such as often found in pre-literate peoples. Their general level of information was pitiful. In fifteen years, I met three young people among my patients who had recently received a British state education who knew the dates of the Second World War, and I thought it a triumph of natural intelligence in the circumstances that one of them deduced from the fact that there had been a Second that there had been a First, though he knew nothing of it. Needless to say, they did not know the date of anything else in history either.

It is true that my patients were a selected sample, and perhaps not representative of the population as a whole;

but my sample was not a small one, and it has to be remembered that it has been proved beyond reasonable doubt that, using the right teaching methods, it is possible to teach nearly 100 per cent of the children coming from the poorest and worst of homes to read and write fluently. This is so, incidentally, even when English is not the language used at home.

It is indicative of the intellectual deformations produced by sentimentality that, when I recounted my experiences to middle-class intellectuals, they imagined that I was criticising or sneering at my patients, rather than drawing attention, with a fury that it required all my self-control not to make absurdly evident, to the appalling injustice done to these children by an educational system that did not even have the advantage (or excuse) of being cheap. Indeed, they largely refused to accept either the truth or the wider validity of my observations, using a variety of mental subterfuges to minimise their significance.

They would say that what I was saying was not true — though all statistical surveys, as well as other anecdotal evidence, suggested that my findings were far from unusual or unique to me. Then they would say that, though true perhaps, it was ever thus, not realising that, even if this were so, it would not justify the present state of affairs. The vast increase in expenditure alone ought to have ensured that what had previously been the case was the case no longer; that previous ages had reasons for not imparting letters to children that were no longer available to us as an excuse for failing to do so; but that, in any case, there was evidence that it was simply not true that it was ever thus.

In France, for example, tests have demonstrated as conclusively as such things can be demonstrated that the level of comprehension of simple written texts, and the ability of today's children to write the French language correctly, has declined by comparison with that of children educated in the 1920s, when controlled for various factors such as social class.[5] Perhaps this is not altogether surprising: when the education correspondent of *Le Figaro* wrote an article drawing attention to declining standards, he received 600 letters from teachers, a third of which contained spelling errors. And it is obvious that among the reasons for the decline in standards in France are the same gimcrack romantic educational ideas that have held sway in Britain for rather longer.

The reluctance of the romantically-inclined to acknowledge that there was something profoundly wrong with an educational system that left a high proportion of the population unable to read properly or do simple arithmetic (despite the expenditure of vast sums and the more than adequate intelligence of that population to master those skills) probably derived from their unwillingness to give up their post-religious sentimentality, the idea that but for the deformations of society, man was good and children were born in a state of grace.

Some of the things written by romantic educational theorists are so ludicrous that it takes a complete absence of sense of humour not to laugh at them, and an almost wilful ignorance of what children, or at least many or most children, are like to believe them. Perhaps my favourite is from Cecil Grant's *English Education and Dr Montessori*, published in 1913:

> No child learning to write should ever be told a letter is faulty... every stupid child or man is the product of discouragement... give Nature a free hand, and there would be nobody stupid.

Clearly Mr Grant was much discouraged in his youth, but not nearly enough, I fear.

Over and over again, the romantics stress the glories of spontaneity. Undirected experience and activity are the means by which children learn best and most, and that their inclination to learn will be quite sufficient. Pestalozzi, the follower of Rousseau, said 'Human powers develop themselves.' The American philosopher and educationist John Dewey, sounding like Harold Skimpole generalising from his own state of mind, wrote during the First World War, 'Force nothing on the child... give it free movement... let it go from one interesting object to another... we must wait for the desire of the child, for consciousness of need.'[6] 'The natural means of study in youth is play,' wrote H. Caldwell Cook, a British educationist from just after the First World War. 'The core of my faith is that the only work worth doing is play; by play I mean doing anything with one's heart in it.'

It would take a long time to disentangle all the patently false assumptions and harmful corollaries (some of them very nasty indeed) of this sentimental drivel. More famous and influential than Cook, however, was Friedrich Froebel who, among other things, wrote:

We must presuppose that the still young human being, even though as yet unconsciously, like a product of nature, precisely and surely wills that which is best for himself, and moreover, in a form quite suitable to him, and which he feels within himself the disposition, power and means to represent.

Froebel, who (to be fair to him) lived before there were electric sockets into which crawling babies were inclined to put their fingers, then goes on to point out that the duckling takes to the water by itself, as the chicken takes to pecking the ground. He enjoins us to look anew on the weeds of the fields, to appreciate that, growing where they listeth, they nevertheless show great beauty and symmetry, 'harmonising in all parts and expressions'. In other words, there are lessons in them there cowslips.

No doubt it will amaze most people that this could have been published, let alone have become influential. But let me here quote from the introductory essay to a book of essays entitled *Friedrich Froebel and English*

Education, published not by one of those niche publishers of books by cranks, but by the London University Press in 1952. The author is Evelyn Lawrence.

> The theoretical battle… rages today, but mainly not among the leaders. Most of them were won over long since, at any rate in the field of the Primary school, and we can safely say that Froebel and his followers played a leading part in such improvement as there has been.

What this meant, in essence, was that, by then, the educationists (those who taught the teachers to teach), but not the teachers themselves, had been won over. For some time yet, the teachers resisted. What now seems almost incredible, as late as 1957 the president of the National Union of Teachers was militating for the teaching of reading, writing and arithmetic along traditional lines.

The romantics also fostered what might be called the Wackford Squeers theory of education, namely that it should be relevant to the lives and practical needs of the pupils.[7] These ideas became enshrined in official thinking much earlier than might suppose, and were not merely the vapourings of innocents, cranks and malcontents. The official Spens report on secondary education in England and Wales, published in 1937, stated that 'the content [of the curriculum] must grow out of, and develop with, the expanding experience of the pupils.' In other words, *relevance* became the touchstone of what was to be taught.

It did not seem to occur to the Spens committee, and many educationists since, that one of the purposes of education is to expand a child's horizons, not to enclose him in whatever little social nutshell fate happens to have enclosed him in.

The Spens report, set up by the Conservative government of the day, demonstrates how quickly the ideas of the educational romantics became a kind of official orthodoxy that initially provoked resistance by those not raised in it, but eventually was unquestioned. In 1931, the same committee had reported on primary education, and in the report of 1937 made reference to its own recommendation:

> The Primary School curriculum should be thought of in terms of activity and experience rather than knowledge to be acquired and facts to be stored.

The committee then went a step further:

> The principle we quote is no less applicable at the later than at the earlier stages.

This leaves open the question of the age or stage of human existence in an advanced economy at which the acquisition of knowledge and facts (among which are such things as the knowledge of how to read and add up) become important and takes precedent over playing in the sandpit. With such an educational philosophy having become prevalent if not quite universal, it is scarcely any wonder that universities complain that they have to teach remedial mathematics, that many newly-qualified doctors think that the word 'lager' (a very important one, considering how many of their patients come to them as a result, direct or indirect, of a surfeit thereof) is spelt 'larger,' or that some teachers of history at Oxford have been officially enjoined not to mark down papers because of errors of spelling or grammar (perhaps because, if they did, very few students would get a degree).

The Spens report is a rich source of sentimentality. 'We think,' concluded the members, 'too much of education in terms of knowledge and too little in terms of feeling and taste.' The idea that feeling and taste cannot be educated in the absence of knowledge and guidance is one that was entirely lost on the authors of the most influential report on English education in the Twentieth century.

Elsewhere, the report says things that contain an element of truth, but are easily overemphasised by the romantic sentimentalists. Pointing out that not everything can be taught by precept, the report says:

A boy may write better English if he has discovered the principles of English composition for himself than if he has merely learnt these principles from a teacher or textbook.

It is, of course, perfectly true that one would not expect a child given a list of precepts of composition[8] to compose well, just by virtue of having memorised them and tried by his own to put them into practice, so that his first work of prose would be first rate. This is not how so complex a skill as writing is learnt: but extremists have taken words such as the above to mean that every child should discover everything for himself, from the principles of composition to Newton's laws of motion and the germ theory of disease. Again, the Spens report is *partly* right in saying that 'a great part of the final elements of a liberal education are as a rule acquired in [an] incidental and unconscious fashion,' but that in no way absolves schools of the responsibility for imparting the skills and knowledge to children to enable the 'incidental and unconscious fashion' to work on something other than a vacuum. Every good teacher has always known that education is more than drilling a certain number of undesired facts into a child's head; but every good teacher has also known that there are things that a child must be taught and come to know that he would never discover for himself, either from inability or disinclination.

It is worth quoting the Spens report at some length to show how the romantic sentimentality took over the official mind much earlier than I, for one, had previously supposed:

We wish to reaffirm a view expressed in our Report on *The Primary School* (1931), in which we urge that *the curriculum 'should be thought of in terms of activity and experience rather than of knowledge to be acquired and facts to be stored'*. Learning in the narrower sense must no doubt fill a larger place in the secondary than in the primary school, but the principle we quote is no less applicable at the later than at the earlier stage. To speak of secondary school studies as 'subjects' is to run some risk of thinking of them as bodies of facts to be stored rather than as modes of activity to be experienced;[9] and while the former aspect must not be ignored or even minimised, it should, in our opinion, be subordinate to the latter. This remark applies most clearly to 'subjects' such as the arts and crafts and music, to which we attach great importance, but which have generally been relegated to an inferior place in the school programme; but upon our view it holds good also of more purely intellectual activities, such as the study of science or mathematics. An unfortunate effect of the present system of public examinations is that it emphasises, perhaps inevitably, the aspect of school studies which we deem to be the less important.

Furthermore:

> … the timetable is overcrowded and congested, and leaves too little time to consider and discuss the wide implications of the subject matter with a consequent limitation of the ability to think.

Years later it is common for it to be thought that the possession of an opinion on a subject, which is active, is deemed more important than having any information on that subject, which is passive; and that the vehemence (feeling) with which an opinion is held is more important than the facts (knowledge) upon which it is based. Of course facts are not everything, Mr Gradgrind notwithstanding.[10] It is common experience that the best informed people on a subject may miss its point entirely, while less-informed persons may grasp it immediately. But the development of a sense of proportion that makes this feat possible requires a mind well-supplied with knowledge of the world, both implicit and explicit. A mind empty of all facts is hardly in a position to view any question in perspective.

Even great minds have sometimes succumbed to the temptation of sentimentality about children: there are passages from John Locke's *Some Thoughts Concerning Education*, of 1690, that would give comfort to the sentimentalists:

> ... they [children] should seldom be put about doing even those things you have got an inclination in them to do, but when they have a mind and disposition to it. He that loves reading, writing, musick, etc., finds yet in himself certain seasons wherein those things have no relish to him; and if at that time he forces himself to it, he only pothers

and wearies himself to no purpose. So it is with children. This change of temper should be carefully observ'd in them, and the favourable seasons of aptitude and inclination be heedfully laid hold of: And if they not often enough forward of themselves, a good disposition should be talk'd into them, before they be set upon any thing.

As for the great poets, though not great thinkers, they too have weighed in on the side of the romantics and sentimentalists:

The mind of Man is fram'd even like the breath
And harmony of music. There is a dark
Invisible workmanship that reconciles
Discordant elements and makes them move
In one society.

Thus Wordsworth in *The Prelude* of 1805. There doesn't seem much left for education to do.

Initially there was some common-sense resistance to the romantic point of view, as a school inspector for Manchester implied in 1950 when she wrote:

The teacher is torn between outside opinion... that of the parents and the general taxpaying public who expect a child to read and work during school hours... and her own knowledge that the child learns best through play.[11]

* * *

But the experts had their way in the end, as they usually do, even though their 'knowledge' that the child learns best through play could not possibly have been as the result of any experience.

An unexpected and powerful contemporary ally of educational romanticism, and sentimentality, is contemporary linguistics, a supposedly scientific discipline. The *locus classicus* of the sentimental (and politically correct[12]) conclusions drawn from the science of linguistics is Steven Pinker's book *The Language Instinct*. Almost certainly, this is the most influential book on the subject ever written, reprinted dozens of times; and since it may be assumed that those who read it are at the upper end of the educational spectrum, it may be assumed to have had an effect.

It draws unjustified and noxious conclusions from what may very well be a correct view of the development of language in individual children.

The part of the theory that may be correct is this: that children are biologically pre-ordained to develop language, that their brains are genetically determined and constructed in such a fashion that, at a certain stage in their lives, they develop language. Furthermore, the language they develop will be rule-governed, and this applies whatever language they learn, whether it be the argot of the slums, the drawl of the aristocrat, or the chatter of women at a Sahelian well.

So far, so good. This may all be so. The evidence

suggests that, if for reasons of social isolation, a child has not learned to talk by the age of six, he will never learn to talk adequately, suggesting that the acquisition of language is indeed biologically programmed.

But then further unjustified and dangerous conclusions are drawn. Since all children learn language spontaneously, a language that is moreover as obedient to grammatical rules as any other language and one that by definition is suited to and adequate for life in the society in which they grow up, no special training in their native language is necessary. This is because no form of language is inherently superior to any other. Language, says Professor Pinker, is not a cultural artifact at all, and therefore cannot be taught. Prescriptive grammar is a 'hobgoblin of the schoolmarm'; a standard language (such as the one in which he himself writes) is a language 'with an army and navy.'[13] All references to standard language and to prescriptive grammar in the book are derogatory, though sometimes infused with a hint of irony, the kind of irony that a metropolitan sophisticate uses when speaking to or of a naïve, unsophisticated and ignorant farm labourer. Among other reasons a standard language should not be taught is that the standard language itself changes with time; what is deemed 'correct' usage today is deemed 'incorrect' tomorrow,[14] so is not worth learning. It is so much wasted effort; the very fact of change undermines the claim to correctitude.

In Pinker's view, at least as expressed in his book though not as expressed in his life, there are no mute inglorious Miltons resting in country churchyards, because everyone spontaneously develops the language that is adequate to his needs. And therefore, as he says at the beginning of his book, quoting Oscar Wilde, 'nothing that is worth knowing can be taught.'

As it happens, there is a great deal of moral exhibitionism in this, an invitation to the reader to exclaim, 'Goodness, how broadminded and democratic this clever and highly-educated man is!' But it is also profoundly insincere. It is highly unlikely that he would wish his own children to grow up speaking only what he calls Black English Vernacular, the adequacy of whose expressiveness he elsewhere extols; and when I wrote an article attacking his view of the matter, pointing out that, among other things, his view, if taken seriously, necessarily enclosed people in the mental worlds into which they had been born, he replied 'Of course people should be taught a standard language.' This proved that he had either changed his mind on the matter (how else they were to be taught than by the much-derided schoolmarms he did not condescend to explain), or that he had never really believed what he had written in the first place.

This is further suggested by the very dedication of his book, which reads: 'For Harry and Roslyn Pinker who gave me language.'

If Professor Pinker was grateful because they gave him language in the purely biological sense, he might as well have written 'For Harry and Roslyn Pinker who gave me urine' or 'For Harry and Roslyn Pinker who gave me faeces,' which are just as biological as language and perhaps even more biologically necessary.[15] But I don't think he did mean this.

In fact, he is simply giving a new, supposedly scientific gloss to old romantic conceits about childhood, conceits that are almost certainly at heart a denial and repudiation of the religious doctrine of Original Sin. I need not recapitulate the apostolic succession of romantic educationists here (Rousseau, Pestalozzi, Froebel, Montessori, Dewey, Steiner, say nothing of their acolytes), but will confine myself to quoting one of Professor Pinker's intellectual — or perhaps, more accurately, emotional — forebears, the social reformer Margaret Macmillan. She did much good, especially for the physical well-being of children, but much harm also; she wrote 'Early childhood is a vital and momentous period in education but it is not the time for accuracy...' By the extension of her principles down the ever-slippery slope, the time for accuracy was never to arrive.[16] Recently, for example, an academic was reported in *The Times* to have suggested that certain spelling errors were now so common among pupils and students that the time had come to accept them as correct, the pupils and students being incorrigible. The academic used every Pinkerian argument: that the errors did not make the meaning of the words indecipherable, that spellings changed anyway over time, etc. etc. Perhaps unsurprisingly, the academic's discipline was criminology, for criminologists have long been to crime what Marshal Petain was to Hitler.

(Professor Pinker's main innovation was the suggestion that, where language was concerned, there was no such thing as accuracy; or, if there was, everyone achieved it merely by virtue of vociferating.)

Professor Pinker tells us that people talk as spiders spin webs, though he is not so foolish as to concede that there are differences; but he also implies that genius inheres in all of us. He does this by quoting the anthropological linguist Edward Sapir, who wrote, 'When it comes to linguistic form, Plato walks with the Macedonian swineherd, Confucius with the head-hunting savage of Assam.' A three year-old, says Professor Pinker, is a grammatical genius. We are all equal, and equal to the best: and all without any training, let alone effort!

In the circumstances, it is hardly surprising that some have come to the conclusion that not only does training and education *per se* fail to promote good, it does active harm by inhibiting the natural genius and creativity of children. Here is Margaret Macmillan again:

The whole question of mind development is concerned in the various kinds of movement natural to, or imposed upon, children... Imagination is of motor origin... Children... learn to read, to write... but not to initiate, to adapt their resources freely. Shakespeare... Bunyan.... where are they today?

Now everyone knows that Shakespeare was a man of

small Latin and less Greek: but the word is small, not non-existent. If he went to Stratford Grammar School he would almost certainly have received a training that was rigorous to the point of cruelty, but which obviously filled his mind with something useful.

The idea that training and knowledge are inimical to the natural genius that inheres in us all has spread to some surprising places.[17] While I was still practising as a doctor, I had a number of patients who were art students. I asked them whether they ever went to art galleries, and they said that they did not. They expected their natural talent to flourish unaided by the inhibitions induced by formal training or by acquaintance with the efforts of past artists: indeed, it was their definition of talent that it should spring spontaneously from their well of genius. Total originality, total disconnection from anything that anyone had ever done before, was their goal, and not surprisingly transgression was their means.

Those young people who said they wanted to be journalists were much the same. Asked what they read, they found the question puzzling: did I not realise that they wanted to be writers, not readers? The notion that writers needed to read was to them very strange. Surely to do so would destroy their originality?

There has, it is true, been a belated reaction to the natural consequences of what one might call 'the play way' or 'feeling' way of education. The attempt to fill minds otherwise innocent of information has resulted in indoctrination with sentimentalism. The only chemical of which children have heard is carbon dioxide because it is a greenhouse gas; they want to save the planet though they can't find China on a map or define a contour. They know that history has been a struggle between oppressor and oppressed because the historical episodes of which they are aware are the Atlantic Slave Trade and the Holocaust (not necessarily in that order). Recently, I met a young woman who was going to university to study history. I asked her what she was learning about and she replied that she was 'doing' the genocide in Rwanda. Swallowing my doubts as to whether so recent an event should form part of the history curriculum for someone who might very well not be able to put the English, American, French and Russian Revolutions in chronological order, I asked her what she had read on the subject? Having myself once travelled through Rwanda, I had read a more than average amount on the subject, and I was curious. It turned out that the one source she could name was the film, *Hotel Rwanda*. I asked her what she thought of the situation in Burundi, Rwanda's southern neighbour that is something of a mirror-image of Rwanda. She hadn't heard of it, nor was she aware that both countries had been Belgian mandated territories (let alone the fact that they had been German colonies before that). Thus it appeared to me that the history she was being taught was a form of sentimental moralising, a kind of declaration of personal virtue to the effect that killing lots of people for no good reason is wrong, a lesson that, even these days, hardly needs teaching since no one would argue otherwise. I do not mean to say that the Rwandan genocide is not a subject for deep moral and psychological reflection; obviously it is. But there is a cheapness of its use here that means the difference between narrative history and soap opera is virtually effaced.

The triumph of the romantic view of education was doubly disastrous because it coincided with the triumph of the romantic view of human relations, especially family relations. This view goes something like this: the object of human life being happiness, and the fact that many marriages are unhappy being patent and obvious, it is time to found human relationships not upon such extraneous and unromantic bases as social obligation, financial interest, and duty, but upon nothing other than love, affection and inclination. All attempts at stability founded upon anything but love, affection and inclination are inherently oppressive and therefore ought to be discounted. Once relations — especially those between the sexes — were founded upon love alone, the full beauty of the human personality, hitherto obscured by clouds of duty, convention, social shame and the like, would emerge, as a shimmering dragonfly in the summer.

And about as long-lasting too. The family, with all its undoubted miseries (as well, of course, as joys) has long been the object of hate of ambitious intellectuals, for the family stands between the state, to be directed by intellectuals, and total power. Claiming to want to bring about a world of joys only, without miseries, intellectuals have almost systematically denigrated the family, taking its worst aspects for the whole, and using reform (often much needed) as a stalking-horse for destruction. Indeed, in Britain, what the Hungarian communists called *salami tactics* have been employed, until marriage, except for those few who are still deeply religious, has been virtually emptied of its moral, social, practical and contractual content. Not surprisingly, the state has entered the breach: a half of the British population is now in receipt of subventions from it in one form or another.

Bernard Shaw (not coincidentally an equal-opportunity admirer of Mussolini, Hitler and Stalin) said that marriage was legalised prostitution; his master Ibsen, an infinitely better playwright, of course, had a heroine whose heroism consisted in part — but generally unnoticed by the audience — of abandoning her own children without so much as a moment's thought as to what it might be like for them.

This turned out to be profoundly prophetic, at least as far as Britain is concerned.[18] For every patient who said to me that he was remaining with the mother of their children for the children's sake, I must have heard a hundred say 'It's just not working' or 'I need my space.' The children's welfare simply does not enter into consideration at all.

The loosening of the bonds between the parents of children, however they were forged, has had disastrous consequences both for individuals and society. So, obviously, one would need to be a trained intellectual to be able to deny them. In the area in which I worked, in a city in which, incidentally, most social indicators such as income and unemployment were more or less average for the country as a whole, it was almost unknown for a child to be living in a household with both of its biological parents. When asked who his or her father was, a young person would often reply 'Do you mean my father at the moment?' Contact with biological fathers had often been completely lost; or, if maintained, was wholly conflictual, since he used it as a weapon in the love-hate war against the mother. Half-siblings were much more common than full siblings; serial step-fatherhood was the norm, and it was far from uncommon for a young mother to expel her own children from her home because her new boyfriend did not wish the children (biological evidence, after all, of her previous liaisons) to remain there, and gave her an ultimatum: them or me. In most cases of which I am aware, the mother chose him, and I do not recall a single case of a woman throwing out the new boyfriend because he demanded the expulsion of her children by other men.

Perhaps all would have been well if some means had been found of reconciling the two sentimental demands of the romantic conception of relations between the sexes: on the one hand that they should be founded on nothing but attraction, sexual desire and affection, and on the other that there should be a great passion at all time between them (anything less making life not worth living). Unfortunately, however, free love and exclusive sexual possession of another person are fundamentally incompatible principles. Nothing can reconcile them.

No one can seriously doubt that under what might now be called the *ancien régime* of sexual relations — in which the normal was taken to be monogamous marriage — there was frustration, unhappiness and hypocrisy. Indeed, if you removed the subject of frustration, unhappiness and hypocrisy from literature, there might be very little left of literature. Adultery was common, and if DNA testing had been available, it would have suggested that a percentage of children of supposedly monogamous marriages were the offspring of other liaisons. A lot was swept under the carpet; not only did a lot go on that was unobserved, but there was also a willingness, that was often difficult to distinguish from a necessity, to overlook the obvious. Divorce and separation were the exception rather than the rule; I remember the time — we might as well be talking about the second millennium BC — when divorcees were spoken of in a special, rather hushed tone of voice.[19]

Nothing excites the mind of reformers like hypocrisy and inconsistency, especially when they themselves are strongly in the grip of the Skimpolian desire to be as free as the butterflies.[20] Away with hypocrisy! Away with frustration! Away with hidden desires! Away with resisted temptation! Let us henceforth live as we wish, without the deformations brought about by furtiveness, let us live in the open! Let the whole of life, indeed, be an open book, so that appearance from now on equals reality!

Now a realist, but not a sentimentalist,[21] would have

known all along that the only way to eliminate hypocrisy from human existence is to abandon all principles whatsoever; and that it is impossible for human beings, with their extremely complex minds that are nevertheless not able fully to understand (because no explanation of anything is ever final) a single one of their own actions, to live completely in the open. A single, and simple, thought experiment is sufficient to establish that complete openness, even if possible, would not be desirable.

Suppose it were possible to produce a thought scanner, a machine that at a distance was able to translate the physiological activity of a person's brain into the thoughts that he was thinking so that, by possessing such an instrument, it was possible for everyone to know what everyone else was thinking. Would one expect the murder rate to go up or down, or any associations between people to endure beyond a few seconds? Such a world would make North Korea seem like a libertarian paradise.

Criticism of a dispensation because it necessitates hypocrisy and concealment, then, is no criticism of it at all. The question, rather, should be what dispensation and what types of hypocrisy and concealment are the least damaging to human well-being? And the problem is compounded by the fact that human beings do not change very fast, at least in all directions: that, for example, you couldn't get rid of the desire for the exclusive sexual possession of another as you could get rid of the impediments to divorce and other pillars of the old dispensation.

Suffice it to say that, at least for a very considerable part of the population, especially the poorest and most vulnerable part, the new dispensation has brought liberty in certain directions, but also the kind of fear, jealousy, violence and general social breakdown that severely circumscribes liberty in much more important directions.

The response to the affective chaos that the new dispensation has brought about falls into two main patterns, which are not however wholly mutually exclusive: namely, overindulgence on the one hand and neglect and abuse on the other.

Often parents, by their own lights good parents, would come to me to ask why their son or daughter had turned out so bad: so moody, aggressive, violent and criminal. They found this difficult to understand because, in their words, 'We gave him (or her) everything.'

When asked what they meant by everything, they replied, give or take a material possession or two, 'The latest trainers, an iPod, a CD player.'[22] Moreover, they had provided these indispensable accoutrements of a happy childhood as and when they were wanted, often at considerable sacrifices to themselves, since they were not rich.

Clearly they were in the grip of the romantic notion that, to paraphrase Blake, it was better to murder an infant in the cradle than to allow him to nurse unacted desires. This fatuously sentimental idea, with its blind refusal to see that acting on desires can sometimes lead precisely to the murder of an infant in the cradle, not to mention other horrors, is now very widespread. It comes as a genuine shock to parents of children to whom nothing has been denied that they should turn out selfish, demanding and intolerant of the slightest frustration.

An additional motive for over-indulgence towards children is the guilt felt by adults who, by acting on their desires, have brought emotional chaos into children's lives. They seek to compensate for this by the gift of material possessions.[23] Needless to say, this is not entirely against the economic interests of a consumerist society.

Among better-off parents, over-indulgence of children's desires for material possessions is often an attempted compensation for a lack of care and attention of, and time devoted to, their own children: in short, a manifestation of bad conscience.

The other side of the coin of over-indulgence is aggressive neglect and violence. It is not necessary to believe the explanations of the neo-Darwinists and sociobiologists to accept that step-parents are many times more likely to be violent to, or sexually abuse, their charges than are biological parents.[24] This has been recognised from time immemorial; it is not for nothing that the step-mother of fairy tales is wicked.

Therefore, he who promotes step-parenthood in society promotes neglect of and violence towards children. This is even more the case when (as is now often the case) step-fatherhood is serial. If, shall we say, one step-father in five is neglectful of or violent towards his stepchildren, then those children who have three stepfathers in their lives (and they are by no means a few in contemporary Britain) have a sixty per cent chance of experiencing neglect or violence in their childhood.

The adults who, despite having brought children into the world, form and break couples like glass being shattered by a stone are themselves acting upon the sentimental theory that unacted upon desires are exceedingly dangerous. This view has been reinforced by a debased Freudianism, a tributary that pours its treacle into the great swamp of modern sentimental sludge and slime. Everyone, even someone who knows nothing of Freud and to whom the word psychoanalysis is meaningless, has heard by now that secret desires and hidden traumas that remain secret and hidden cause severe problems later in life. When I asked an English football supporter who, along with ten thousand others, had travelled to Italy to watch a supposedly friendly game between Italy and England why he had come all this way to shout vile obscene abuse at the Italians (I was at the time what might be called the vulgarity correspondent of a newspaper, which would ask me to go to places where the English gathered *en masse* to behave badly, which in effect was everywhere they gathered *en masse*) he replied, 'You have to let your hair down.' Like most of the other ten thousand he was thoroughly middle class.

Likewise, if you ask young people why they drink themselves to extinction, again *en masse*, making a public exhibition or nuisance of themselves on the way, they will reply that it is necessary for them to lose all their inhibitions to express themselves, as if what was within them to express were pus that would accumulate in an abscess if they did not express it, and give them the emotional equivalent of septicaemia.[25] As the English working class used to say of their teeth, which they knew would all go rotten before long and give rise to severe pain, better out than in.

Hence if a relationship between a man and a woman had its difficulties — if, in the pseudoconfessional way of speaking about oneself that has become almost universal, 'it (that is to say the relationship) just isn't going anywhere' — there was only one possible recourse that would avoid the terrible *dénouement* brought about by frustration and unhappiness, namely separation, regardless of the interests of the children of the relationship. And, as we have seen, the government has thoughtfully ensured that no material interests, at least at the lower end of the socio-economic spectrum, could stand in the way of this happy outcome.

The extreme fragility and friability of relations between the sexes combined with the persisting desire for the exclusive sexual possession of another leads, not unnaturally, to a great deal of jealousy, which itself is the most common and powerful reason for violence between the sexes. This has been so for a long time. For example, the prison psychiatrist, Dr Norwood East, found in a survey published in 1949 that 46 of 200 non-insane murderers killed from motives of sexual jealousy, the joint most common motive and nearly as many again as those who killed for pecuniary motives.

It is obvious why the friability of relationships should promote jealousy (so long as the desire for the exclusive sexual possession of another, which shows no sign of declining, remains). Just as, in the field of employment, easy fire means easy hire, so a relationship that has started casually can end casually. Most men think that other men are like themselves, and in any given social milieu that is likely to be more or less true; so if they are sexually predatory, and if, as is often the case, they have 'poached' the sexual partner of their best friend, they suppose that everyone around them, including their friends or so-called friends, is engaged upon the same course of action. This has two consequences: a way must be found to keep the object of their desires away from the hands and often even the gaze of others, there being no better way of achieving this, at least in the short term, than arbitrary violence, for such violence is so preoccupying that the 'loved' one has no time or energy for extracurricular activities; and second, it gives rise to the who-you-looking-at-culture, in which every other male is a potential sexual predator. Prevention being better than cure, a glass in the face is better than a further opportunity to catch the eye, and arouse the concupiscence, of the loved one.

In summary, then, the sentimental view of childhood and relations between the sexes has the following consequences.

It leaves many children unable to read properly and perform simple calculations. This in turn results in enclosing such children in the social conditions in which they find themselves at birth, for an inability to read, and a poor basic education, are almost (though perhaps not quite) impossible to rectify later in life. Not only does this mean that talent may be wasted and intelligent children and adults left deeply frustrated, but it lowers the general level of culture of society. The notion that human relations ought to be permanently and passionately blissful, and therefore that every social, contractual, economic and customary obstacle to the achievement of this end ought to be removed, thereby eliminating every source of frustration and motive for hypocrisy, leads to overindulgence, neglect of and violence towards children, as well as an increase in levels of jealousy, the most powerful of all motives for violence between the sexes.

The romantic and sentimental view of the most important aspects of human existence are therefore intimately connected to the violence and brutality of daily life, which has almost certainly worsened in Britain over the last sixty years, notwithstanding the immense improvements in levels of physical comfort and well-being.

It remains to be pointed out that one of the consequences of the general adoption of the romantic and sentimental view of human existence is a blurring of boundaries between the permissible and the impermissible: for life itself decrees that not everything is or can be permissible. It is simply impossible to live as if it were true that it is better to strangle babies than let them, or anyone else, have unacted desires.[26] But the blurring of boundaries occasioned by the adoption of an impossible view as if it were true, and the consequent refusal of individuals to accept limitations on their own lives imposed by extraneous forces, that is to say forces that are independent of their will or whim, such as social convention, contract and the like, means that uncertainty becomes not the province of intellectual speculation, but of the very way that life should be lived. Uncertainty, by means of reaction against it, breeds intolerance and violence.

Nowhere is this seen more clearly than in the question of sexuality and childhood. Assuming that there must be a legal age of consent to sexual relations, the fact remains that any age that is chosen must, to an extent, be arbitrary. It is absurd to suppose that, if it is sixteen, a child of 15 years and 364 days actually and in reality has matured one day later to such an extent that he or she is capable of deciding what he or she was previously incapable of deciding. The same would be true of any age chosen.

From this it seems to be the case that what is legally impermissible may nonetheless be morally and practically permissible — at least, that is the conclusion that has been drawn by most people in our society. A fifteen year-old cannot legally consent to sexual relations, and all such relations are therefore criminal; but doctors are enjoined to prescribe even younger children with contraceptives without informing their parents, publications designed for eleven and twelve year-olds are often an explicit invitation to sexual behaviour, and there is no doubt whatever that many parents connive at the illegal sexual activities of their children. It is true that some men are still convicted of having had sexual intercourse with girls who were under the age of consent, but they often claim, not wholly implausibly, that the girls in question did not look their age and were allowed by their parents out at a time when one would not expect girls of such an age to be allowed out (in the general drunken and drug-fuelled sexual *sauve-qui-peut* that takes place in the centre of British town and city every Friday and Saturday night it is hardly to be expected that inspection of birth certificates should be demanded and accorded). Furthermore, the men claim that they are being punished not so much for having had sexual intercourse with such girls, but in effect for stopping having had sexual relations with such girls: the girls being unhappy at the cessation, they run to their parents — who already knew of the relations — and ask that they should go to the police. The convicted men feel aggrieved not because they are innocent of the charge, but because they have only done what many others have done and continue to do, with the knowledge and even approval of the parents of the girls. The age of consent thus becomes not a rule to be obeyed, but a weapon to be wielded.

More importantly, the social conditions in which sexual abuse of children is most likely to occur have been assiduously promoted first by intellectuals and then by the state. And those with a guilty conscience often seek a scapegoat by means of which to expiate themselves.

The current scapegoat in Britain for the neglect and abuse of children that is consequent upon the refusal of the population to place a limit on its own appetites (to quote Burke), is paedophilia. This is not to deny the seriousness of paedophilia: I am not sure whether the supply creates the demand or the demand the supply, but there can be little doubt of the horrors committed against children so that images of what is done to them may be sold over the internet. In the nature of things, it is difficult to know whether the worst forms of paedophilia are on the increase or not; but the fact remains that a child is vastly more likely to be abused at home, by a member of the household or at least a frequent visitor to the household, than by anyone else. And millions of people have contributed to the maximisation of the chances.

And so it is to paedophiles and paedophilia that the guilty hysteria of the population is directed. So great has it become that on one infamous occasion a paediatrician's house was stoned by a mob, paediatrics and paedophilia being indistinguishable to them.[27] In Britain, scenes outside courts of mob hostility towards alleged paedophiles who are being brought to appear there (the notion that a man is innocent until proven guilty being completely alien to the mob) have become quite common; and women, often with a terrified child in tow, scream abuse and even hurl missiles at the vehicles containing the alleged malefactor, apparently unaware that to expose a child to such scenes is abusive. It is a racing certainty that most of the women who behave in this way live in the very circumstances that are most likely to give rise to the sexual abuse of children. Were it not for the presence of the police, it is likely that in such scenes torture followed by a lynching might very well take place.

The connection between sentimentality and lynch law is further demonstrated by the violence of prisoners towards their co-detainees who are guilty of (or merely on remand for) sexual offences.[28] The rationale for this violence is that the sex offenders 'interfere with little kiddies' — always little kiddies, by the way, and never mere children. The authorities have to protect the offenders from the sentimental wrath of men who, not infrequently, have themselves caused a great deal of misery to others and acted brutally, and who are great getters and neglecters of children.

Sentimentality is the progenitor, the godparent, the midwife of brutality.

1

Sentimentality

Recently I went into a branch of WH Smith in a small market town in rural England. The choice of books was not large or impressive, to say the least; there was nothing that could remotely be called a classic for sale. The townsfolk were evidently not intellectual in their interests. On the other hand, there was a comparatively large section devoted to a literary genre of which I had previously overlooked: Tragic Life Stories.

I was aware of a new literary genre of writing about the experience of illness. An American magazine once sent me seven books in the genre for review all at once, including a middle-aged woman's account of her colostomy. This book was not intended as practical advice for those unfortunate people who themselves were about to undergo a colostomy: it is easy enough to see the need for such a book. If I were myself about to have a colostomy, I should find the experience of others helpful in guiding me through what must be a difficult and painful transition. No; this book was intended for the general, that is to say the uncolostomised, public. Many folk nowadays, it seems, like nothing more than to read of the illnesses of others: for when the small change of other people's lives is projected into the public sphere, in writing or on television, it reassures everyone of the significance of his own life. Importance has been democratised, or at least demoticised: we are all important now.

In America, this literary genre is called *Life Writing*, and it is possible to take entire university courses in it. In English departments the study of writing about colostomies and the like evidently takes its place as a worthy subject beside Restoration Comedy and the Nineteenth Century Novel. A friend of mine, who was the last person to see Sylvia Plath alive before she committed suicide, sent me the programme of a colloquium on the poet she was invited to attend in Oxford, and among the papers was one by an American professor who had 'used postmodern theories of embodiment to examine contemporary literary representations of breast, uterine and ovarian cancer.'

But until my visit to WH Smith in the market town to which I have referred above, I was completely unaware of the existence of the literary genre of Tragic Life Stories. I was aware of such life stories themselves, of course; indeed, in my medical practice I had encountered very little else, even if people had contributed a great deal to their own tragedies. Without tragedy, moreover, literature would be much impoverished, perhaps even non-existent, since the need for it would vanish.

Yet I had never seen books classified in this way before, and the novelty of the arrangement surely tells us something about our present Zeitgeist, as does the classification of books by the race, sex or sexual practices of their authors.

The titles of the books in the Tragic Life Stories section also tells us something about what a substantial number of people, at least, are now seeking in their leisure moments. (I assume, of course, that WH Smith know what their customers want, which may not be the case. Large companies are bureaucracies, and bad decisions are hidden in the overall results.) Here, however, is a selection of the titles:

Please, Daddy, No
Twilight Children
Daddy's Little Girl: A mother who didn't love her enough, a father who loved her too much
Last Song of the Last Tram: A heart-warming, heartbreaking memoir of a mother's love and a father's abuse
Fragile
Someone to Watch Over: The true tale of a survivor haunted by the demons of abuse
Alone: the heartbreaking story of a neglected child

My Name Is Angel: A traumatic story of escaping the streets and building a new life

Heartland: How a lonely child came to fall in love with a monster

Running from the Devil: How I survived a stolen childhood

The Little Prisoner: How a childhood was stolen and a trust betrayed

The Step Child: A story of a broken childhood

Hidden: Betrayed, exploited and forgotten

Daddy's Challenge: The true story of a father learning to love his son

Such a Pretty Girl: They promised Meredith nine years of safety but only gave her three

Abandoned: A little girl desperate for love

Behind Closed Doors: A true story of neglect and survival against the odds

Don't Tell Mummy: A true story of the ultimate betrayal

Our Little Secret: A father's abuse, a son's life destroyed

Little Girl Lost: A powerful true story of surviving the unimaginable

Not entirely by coincidence, I suspect, the Tragic Life Stories section was immediately next to the section devoted to True Crime. Here, if anywhere, was an elective affinity. After all, having tragic life stories to weep over depends, is parasitic, upon the brutality of those who make the life stories tragic in the first place. Whereas the covers of the Tragic Life Stories (many of which, incidentally, were in their nth printing) were predominantly of boudoir-pastel shades, with pictures of a little child on them covering his or her tearful or imploring face, the covers of the True Crime were in lurid and diabolic red and black, and had pictures staring out of them of brutal shaven-headed men of the type produced in larger numbers in Britain than anywhere else in the world, and indistinguishable incidentally (as a Swedish visitor recently pointed out to me) from the faces that adorn the covers of many a footballer's autobiography. Anyhow, one title will be sufficient, I hope, to give the flavour of the genre:

> *Chopper 6: A bullet in time saves nine (luckily there is a never-ending supply of evil).*

I walked away from WH Smith feeling as if I had immersed myself in a mixture of syrup and blood, and as if I needed a good shower to wash it off. But before I did so, I bought a couple of newspapers, the first local and the second national.

The lead story of the first concerned a father who was angrily demanding an apology from a local supermarket:

> A dad is raging against the town's supermarket after his daughter found a chicken foot in her roast dinner.
>
> His daughter wiped some gravy to the side of her plate and discovered the claw... and burst into tears.

'It got cooked and managed to get on to my daughter's plate. It scared her to death. She won't eat meat at all now.'

'All our dinners were totally wasted.'

'All we used of it was the breast meat so we don't understand how it came to be there.'

'My daughter is 11, she burst out crying, and that was it and everybody's dinners went out the window.'

'We had to throw it all away because there was a bit of an upheaval.'

This little incident is instructive in a number of ways, not least in the extremity of the emotion, or at least in the extremity of the expression of emotion, occasioned by what was at most a very minor unpleasantness (chicken feet, after all, are a delicacy in some cuisines, including those which are vastly more refined than any of which this young girl is likely to have had experience).

But the most significant aspect of the story, assuming it to be true, is that the girl controlled the parents and not the parents the girl. It was she, not they, who determined what happened in the household. Instead of trying to calm her hysteria, either by consolation or by discipline, her parents participated in it and in doing so probably increased it yet further.

In effect, they were transferring the *locus* of moral, intellectual and emotional authority from themselves to their daughter. *Locus*, they conceded that it was she who was the proper judge of how to react to a trivial shock, and that the only way in which they could show their love for her was by reacting in precisely the same way. There was no question of guidance, let alone correction.

Why not? Although a family that collectively throws its dinner out of the window, either metaphorically or literally (and one cannot altogether exclude the latter, to judge by the state of Britain's streets and gardens), at the instigation of some hysterical screaming on the part of an eleven year-old child, is unlikely to reflect deeply or even at all on the way that life should be lived, this does not mean that it escapes the influence of abstract ideas altogether, which it absorbs in inchoate fashion. And among those ideas is likely to be the supposed inherent, spontaneous goodness of children when they have not yet been deformed and corrupted by social training, as well as the vital necessity of the outward, visible and audible, expression of emotion. To have demanded of the child that she should control herself, that she try to see the situation in some kind of proportion and behave accordingly for the sake of decorum and the convenience of others, would therefore have been to inhibit her, to turn her emotion dangerously inwards. Since children are inherently and by nature good, they and not adults are the ultimate moral authorities, though on one very important condition: that they have not been taught artificially to control themselves. Furthermore, the only way in which one can demonstrate true sympathy with another person, including one's own child, is by seeing things from exactly his or her point of view, in so far as seeing it from any other point of view is, potentially at least, a criticism. And only monsters of intolerance judge other people, whatever their age.

Needless to say, consistency of world outlook is not to be looked for in even the most studious and logically scrupulous of intellectuals, let alone in the defenestrators of dinners, and it is possible that there were other strands in the reaction of the parents to the supposed distress of their child. Why, for example, did the father have no difficulty in passing severe moral judgement on the supermarket that sold the chicken with the chicken foot, but make no comment on the carelessness of his wife who, apparently, was responsible for the far grosser and more simply-averted error of serving the said avian extremity up to her daughter? I hope I shall not be accused of cynicism when I suggest that the possibility of reimbursement and even compensation by the supermarket had something to do with the difference in reaction. The father could hardly demand compensation on behalf of his daughter from his wife; but the supermarket, with its immense economic resources, was an easy target for what amounted to moral blackmail.

Every doctor who has prepared reports on people who allege that they have been wrongly or negligently injured by a person or organisation worth suing will have heard the phrase, 'It's ruined my life, doctor.' Of course, lives sometimes genuinely are ruined by the negligence or outright wickedness of others, though in such cases plaintiffs rarely exaggerate for the obvious reason that they don't have to do so. Their lives are genuinely ruined. However, it is a lamentable fact of human nature that, when people have a financial incentive to magnify the distress that they feel, they will magnify it; sometimes for so long, indeed (given the law's delay), that what started out as bogus or at least grossly exaggerated suffering will eventually become real and genuine suffering. Unfortunately, our deeply corrupt — or is it merely sentimental? — system of tort law makes no distinction whatever between these two kinds of suffering, and attributes both to the original injury. Lawyers, after all, need clients, both plaintiffs and defendants, with large sums of money at stake.

In short, the response of the parents to the reaction of their daughter to a very trivial shock (assuming that they were not making the story up from whole cloth) was probably provoked, at least in part, by the hope of 'compo,' that is to say compensation, the modern form of alchemy that transmutes not base metal, but distress, into gold. And motivated exaggeration soon becomes a habit, a whole way of life.

Nor should we underestimate the role of boredom in the production of exaggerated emotion: for what is human life without drama? The scale of a life in which the finding of a chicken foot in a roast chicken (perhaps one day the geneticists will engineer a chicken without feet, thus obviating the problem for supermarkets) may readily be imagined; in such an existence, the throwing of tantrums must stand guarantor of life's significance and meaning.

The article in the local newspaper depended for its effect on readers upon another unspoken, widely-accepted but deeply sentimental notion: namely, that in any conflict between a large organisation and an individual, the organisation must be to blame and the individual must have been maltreated. Now of course we should not fall prey to precisely the opposite, equally sentimental notion, namely that large commercial organisations serve only the public and can do no wrong because they operate in a market place. There are, perhaps, some people who believe this, but they may be swiftly excluded from the kingdom of the sane.

But given that we all have had experience in our daily lives of how cruelly, shabbily and dishonestly human beings, including ourselves, sometimes treat each other as individuals, it is surely stretching credibility to suppose that those same human beings, with all their capacity for greed and mendacity, should suddenly become as pure as the driven snow and as truthful as George Washington in their dealings with large organisations. Yet this is precisely the preposterous premise that the writer of the story assumed that his readers would accept without question.

It is not possible to conclude from the bookshelves of one shop in one small town, or from one story in one minor local newspaper, that an entire country of 60,000,000 inhabitants such as Great Britain is now sunk, or at least is now sinking, in a foetid swamp of sentimentality whose aesthetic, intellectual and moral correlates are dishonesty, vulgarity and barbarity; but if such were the case, as I contend that it is, observation of the fact would have to start somewhere. And it is easier to find confirmatory evidence than to find disconfirmatory evidence. No social phenomenon, however well-attested, is uniform: if I say that the Dutch are now the tallest people in the world, I do not mean that every one of them is well over six feet tall. The response to the bombings in London by Moslem fanatics in July, 2005, was admirably restrained and stoical, in keeping with an earlier tradition; but this does not mean that childish and uncontrolled emotionality is not a growing feature of our national life and character.

Certainly, the transfer of moral authority from adult to child is not confined to impulsive defenestrators of dinners. A semantic shift illustrates this very well. The word 'pupil' is now hardly ever used of children in school; every child is a 'student' from the moment he enters kindergarten. It used to be that the transition from pupil to student was an important one, almost a metamorphosis in fact, or at least a rite of passage. A pupil was highly dependent upon a teacher for what he learnt, who decided what it was necessary for a pupil to learn; by contrast, a student, having mastered certain basic skills and acquired, to an extent by rote, a framework of knowledge laid down for him by his elders and betters, was more self-directed in his learning. He did not acquire independent authority over what he learnt by virtue merely of drawing breath; he acquired it by virtue of certified accomplishment.

A friend of mine was once a teacher of severely mentally handicapped children. His worthy task was to train them to become as independent as possible. He taught them such skills as buttoning up their shirts and putting on their shoes. One day a directive emerged from the local government body that employed him: henceforth, the severely handicapped children were to be known as 'students.'

The directive was simultaneously absurd, grandiose, sentimental, linguistically impoverishing and insulting: not an easy combination to achieve in so short a compass. It was absurd, grandiose and sentimental because it supposed that hard realities — in this case, the profound handicaps of some unfortunate children — could be altered fundamentally and in desirable ways by simple bureaucratic fiat.

The decree was linguistically impoverishing because it made the distinctions between different categories of people slightly more difficult to express. If a fifteen year-old who is laboriously learning to do up his buttons is a student, what are we to call a young man learning physics or classics at university? If he, too, is a student, what will the word student actually convey? Thus a word comes to include too much and mean too little; and thus the habit of insinuating falsehood while suppressing truth is subtly inculcated into a whole population.

The decree was insulting because its ostensible

justification, namely that the use of the word 'student' would increase respect for the severely handicapped, and thereby improve the way in which they were treated, implied that they had been badly treated beforehand, and that the work hitherto done by those subject to the decree was not only defective, but morally defective.

The abandonment of pupil for student is only a slight verbal shift, you may say, of the kind that has always occurred in every language. After all, no language can, does or ought to remain static in its usages. Confucius had the answer to this objection thousands of years ago:

> If language is not correct, then what is said is not what is meant; if what is said is not what is meant, then what must be done remains undone; if this remains undone, morals and art will deteriorate; if justice goes astray, the people will be confused. Hence there must be no arbitrariness in what is said. This matters above everything.

Confucius's proposed reform of language — actually, a return of the original alignment of the denotation of words with their connotation — was in the direction of, and for the purpose of knowing, truth. Modern attempts at language reform, on the other hand, are attempts to bring about a political end, usually utopian and therefore both romantic and sentimental: one that is simultaneously desired — at least is said to be desired — and known not to be possible. It is therefore a permanently useful but dishonest tool for those who seek power. Sentimentality is the ally of megalomania and corruption.

The second newspaper that I bought that day was a famous Sunday periodical, read by many British intellectuals. Its lead story was about the opposition party's plan for education, according to which almost every child, save the severely mentally handicapped, should and would, under its benevolent dictation, be able to read by the age of six.

There are many possible objections, of varying validity, to this proposal, but one, by a member of the National Primary Headteachers' Association, caught my eye. He said, 'One of the worst things you can do with a very young child is give them the impression that they can't do something. That can put them off for a very long time, if not for ever.'

Now these are weasel words, for they are capable of a sentimental interpretation as well as of one that contains a truth. The habit of humiliating children in sadistic fashion in front of their peers for errors that they have made in some task, by telling them that they are too stupid or incapable to do better, is obviously, if not 'one of the worst things you can do with a very young child' (given the very considerable repertoire of human beastliness and cruelty), very bad indeed. It is easy to imagine how such humiliation, especially if it is repeated, might so sap a child's confidence that it gives up trying.

Unfortunately, this rather obvious pedagogical principle has sometimes been extended to the point at which any criticism of the child's efforts is to be eschewed allegedly for the same reason. On this view, it is more important to foster a child's self-esteem (which is self-respect once it has been ideologically sentimentalised) by not marking his work down than to ensure by correcting him that he masters an important skill or piece of knowledge. This supposes that children are psychologically so fragile that they can stand practically nothing in the way of correction, and that they do not derive great pleasure in being able to do well what they formerly were not able to do at all. There is no pleasure in mastery, this ideology claims, but only in uncritical self-satisfaction.

I am not setting up a straw man to knock over with ease. There is little doubt that, despite the expenditure of vast sums on education (four times more per head than in 1950), standards of literacy have not risen in this country and may even have fallen. Certainly, they have fallen at the higher end of the educational spectrum. Not only do employers now complain of graduates who are unable to compose a simple letter; not only did a lecturer at Imperial College recently remark that foreign students often wrote better English — though it was not their first language and was sometimes not even their second, than British students; not only have I noticed that spelling errors are now far more frequently made by doctors in medical notes than previously; but a friend of mine who teaches history at Oxford is specifically enjoined by the guidelines provided for markers by the authorities not to mark students down for their poor grammar, spelling and composition. If he were to so mark them, as once he would have done, good degrees would be awarded far less often than they are awarded. But at least the self-esteem of the students is preserved.

Powerful intellectual currents feed into the great Great Sargasso Sea of modern sentimentality about children. It is hardly necessary to mention the influence of Jean-Jacques Rousseau in this respect. His influence was profound, if hard to quantify with the precision demanded by those who forget Einstein's maxim, that not everything that is measurable is important, while not everything that is important is measurable. Rousseau taught the world what it was only too delighted to hear, namely that man was born good, and that it was only the effects of society that made him bad. In *Emile*, therefore, he advised parents to allow the body of the young child its natural habits, thus 'accustoming him to be always his own master and to follow the dictates of his will as soon as he has a will of his own:' his will, uncontaminated as yet by the deformations of social pressure and convention, always leading him to do what is right. Not only is the news that we are all good by nature extremely gratifying, suggesting that our faults are not really our own at all but attributable to something external to us, but the advice to allow the child always to follow the dictates of its will is extremely convenient for busy, two-income families, in which the parents return home each day in a state of exhaustion, little wanting to deny the little ones their desires in case they start screaming. The proper disciplining of children requires judgment; judgment requires thought; thought requires energy; and everyone is dog-tired. So a permissive rule-of-thumb is just what the doctor ordered. The fact that he who pays the Danegeld never gets rid of the Dane is of small account in the purchase of an hour's much-needed and longed-for peace.

There are other, more recent intellectual sources of sentimentality about children. For example, the Harvard psychologist Steven Pinker, consistently derides in his best-selling book *The Language Instinct* what he calls 'schoolmarms,' that is to say those who believe that the language that children develop spontaneously ought to be refined and corrected, at least if they are to participate in the intellectual life of the world. Pointing out that all children learn language without being taught it, that all forms of language, including the patois of the slums, is bound by grammatical rules of equal regularity, and moreover that all forms of language are capable of expressing abstractions, Pinker comes to the conclusion that those who try to teach children a standard language, such as he himself writes, by means of correction and inculcation, are misguided at best and malicious at worst, knowing or unknowing instruments of the perpetuation of a social hierarchy, since (here he quotes an aphorism famous in the field of linguistics with approval) a standard language is merely a language with an army and navy.

It follows from this that children arrive in school

speaking a language that either is, or spontaneously will become, adequate to their needs, and to amend which is at best pointless and at worst harmful and cruel. Authority over language is thus transferred from adults in general and teachers in particular to children themselves, whose authority in such matters is a natural consequence of the way in which language develops. It need hardly be pointed out that no 'child-centred' idea could be better adapted to ensuring that children in the worst areas of our cities not only remain where they are physically and socially, but mentally too. And child-centredness is a form of sentimentality.

Entering further into the newspaper, one reads, under the headline 'Cardinal Urges Prison Reform,' that the Archbishop of Westminster, Cardinal Cormac Murphy-O'Connor, 'will say today that there has been a shocking increase in prison suicide levels because of prison overcrowding. The system is stretched to breaking point, with the overcrowding crisis making regular headlines in our news bulletins.' His remarks coincide with Prisoners' Sunday, designated a day of reflection and prayer for all those involved in the prison system.'

There had been, it is true, an increase from 67 suicides in prisons in 2006 to 78 such suicides in the first eleven months of 2007. But the figure for 2006 was itself the lowest for ten years, despite an increase in the number of prisoners in total, and also of overcrowding.

There is little doubt that the tendency of the article, and probably its intention, was to arouse a certain emotion — again — whose effect, if not its intention, was to convince the person experiencing it that he was a person of superior sensibility and compassion. How terrible that 78 young men were so distressed that they killed themselves, and how terrible a system that drove them to it! And what a good man I must be to feel so strongly about it! (Since the whole text of what the Cardinal had to say was not provided, but only the words quoted above, it would be unfair to accuse him of anything, except perhaps superficiality in regard to the use of statistics.)

This kind of emotionality often attaches to the question of crime and punishment in contemporary Britain. On the day on which the government announced the construction of a few more prisons, not very long after the Cardinal made his remarks, another newspaper favoured by the intellectual classes ran an entire front page of emotional statistics, with the headline, 'The real prison numbers scandal.' Here are some of the scandalous numbers:

81,455: the prison population of England and
    Wales.
12,275: number of prisoners from ethnic
    minorities
148 per 100,000: the rate of imprisonment in
    England and Wales, the highest in Western
    Europe
64 per cent: the rate of re-offending within two

years of release
76 per cent: the re-offending rate for juvenile
offenders
70 per cent: prisoners who arrive with a drug
problem

The frisson of supposedly virtuous emotion for public display and consumption, or sentimentality, is here created by the deliberate evasion of complexity and the avoidance of thought about unpleasant realities. It would, indeed, take an entire book in itself to unravel all the sentimental evasions contained in this single page of a single newspaper on a single day: rarely have the rhetorical devices of *suppressio veri* (suppression of the truth) and *suggestio falsi* (implying a falsehood) been used in so concentrated a manner.

I will attempt nothing exhaustive: it would also be too exhausting. I shall point out only a few obvious defects of this way of presenting matters (that are all at the service of sentimentality).

The two absolute numbers, of prisoners in England and Wales, and of prisoners who come from ethnic minorities, are given as numerators without any denominators. This suggests that the absolute numbers are more important than the numbers in relation to something else. A moment's reflection should be enough to demonstrate that this cannot possibly be so.

Suppose that no crimes had ever been committed in England and Wales. Suppose also that one man was held in prison. This would be an outrage and a grave injustice, even though the total number of prisoners was extremely low, for the obvious reason that the man held in prison must have been innocent of any crime. This proves what ought to have needed no proof, namely that there is not, and cannot be, a correct or ideal number of prisoners relative to no other consideration. And the other consideration (I apologise for pointing out something so obvious) is the number of crimes committed. Thus, to experience outrage on the basis of an absolute number is to indulge — to self-indulge — in the merest sentimentality.

The same argument applies to the number of people from ethnic minorities who are imprisoned. It is possible, of course, that the figure arises from the racial prejudice or xenophobia of the criminal justice system; but there is nothing in the raw figure alone to prove or even to suggest it. Not only is the proportion of ethnic minorities in the whole population not given, but the proportion and seriousness of the crimes committed by them is not given. A recent report that half the murders committed in London in the last year were committed by foreigners suggests that this is a matter of some statistical importance. But again, the reader is invited to fan the embers of his righteous indignation (which is often sentimentality in its angry phase, and is always gratifying) on the basis of a single absolute number.

Where a denominator is given, it is obviously the wrong one. The example given above can be used again to demonstrate this. If no crimes had ever been committed in England and Wales, yet there were 500 prisoners in the two countries, England and Wales would have not the highest, but the lowest, rate of imprisonment in Western Europe: but I trust everyone would agree that this fact alone would not in any way absolve the criminal justice system of having committed the grossest injustice. A high rate of imprisonment cannot, by itself, constitute evidence of injustice either.

It is obvious, then, that a more informative (and dare I say it, an intellectually more honest) denominator ought to have been used. The figure used should not have been the rate of imprisonment in England and Wales per 100,000 population, but the rate of imprisonment per 100,000 crimes committed, or possibly per 100,000 convictions. With regard to the former, the rate of imprisonment per crimes committed, the figure tells a very different story from the one implied on the front page of the newspaper: England and Wales fall somewhere in the middle of the European range. And if England and Wales imprisoned criminals as they are imprisoned in Spain, for the same reasons, there would not be 80,000 prisoners, but between 350,000 and 400,000 of them.

In other words, Spain has a lower number of prisoners per 100,000 population because it is very much less crime-ridden that Britain. One may argue about the role of imprisonment in keeping it that way; but what one may not say, and ought not to imply, is that the criminal justice system of England and Wales is uniquely harsh or retributive. Once again, a figure has been used to arouse thoughtlessly self-gratifying emotion.

The rate given of re-offending within two years of release applies only to short sentences of a year or less, a fact omitted not by accident.[29] There is strong presumptive evidence, the general dissemination of which the Home Office has done its best to hinder, that the longer the prison sentence the lower the rate of re-conviction. The rate of 64 per cent re-offending is meant automatically to imply to the right-thinking that imprisonment is useless; but a moment's reflection — which one takes for granted will not occur in the minds of the right-thinking — should be sufficient to suggest that the figure is as at least as indicative of the need for longer prison sentences as it is of the uselessness of imprisonment. It is premature release, not imprisonment itself, which is useless or harmful.

There is an omission of a highly-relevant fact that would rather spoil the rhetorical effect of the figure of 64 per cent re-offending rate: namely, that the re-offending figure for all types of non-custodial sentences is as high or higher, even though (one hopes) that those given non-custodial sentences are less dyed-in-the-wool criminals than those given prison sentences, and should therefore be less likely to re-offend. Moreover, while the re-offending rate for those released from prison is calculated from the date of their release, the rate of re-offending for those given non-custodial sentences is calculated from the date when the sentence is first imposed. In other words, officialdom in its presentation of the statistics automatically discounts the protective and preventive effect of imprisonment itself as it is taking place — prisoners being unable to commit offences against the public while they are still in prison. Furthermore, a re-offender weighs equally heavily in the re-offending rate whether he re-offends (that is to say, is caught) only once in two years or a hundred times in two years. It is easy to see, then, that it is highly likely that many hundreds of thousands of crimes a year are committed by convicted criminals who are already serving non-custodial sentences. Indeed, it is known that at least 50 homicides a year are committed by them — homicides that the Archbishop of Westminster might have referred to in his remarks on prison suicides. For if suicide serves to make prison unacceptable, then, by the same token, homicide makes alternatives to prison unacceptable. At the very least, hard thought is necessary to resolve matters; a warm glow of self-congratulatory sentimentality, stoked by statistics that, if not quite false, are selected with the care of a pedigree breeder, is not enough, indeed is a hindrance to such thought.

The implication of the statistic that 70 per cent of prisoners 'arrive [in prison] with a drug problem' is, of course, intended to imply that they are not morally responsible for their crimes because their condition, or illness, 'made' them commit those crimes. No man wants to be, or can help being, ill; seventy per cent of prisoners, therefore, are by definition wrongly imprisoned. How generous-minded of us to acknowledge it and feel outrage at the wrong done to them!

But this view of the matter is thoroughly sentimental. It was Aristotle who said that a man who committed an offence while intoxicated was doubly guilty: first of the offence itself, and second of having intoxicated himself. (This view needs to be somewhat modified or refined. It is within the experience of many doctors that patients have behaved bizarrely or illegally under the influence of a medicament prescribed for them which they had no reason to suppose would cause them to do so. I was once involved in just such a case in which I was disturbed by how little notice the judge appeared to take of the involuntary and unpredictable behavioural effects of a drug that the accused man, of previously good character, had taken at the suggestion of his doctor.)

We are perfectly accustomed to the idea that a man's drunkenness, even if he is an alcoholic, does not excuse his violent behaviour, however much sympathy we may feel for him as a man once he is sober. Why should we think that people with 'drug problems' should be dealt with differently from drunks?

Moreover, if the argument is that a man cannot help his misdeeds and criminal acts because of the illness from which he suffers (laudable conduct, of course, is rarely explained as if it has an outside cause, which suggests that we now believe that the inherent goodness of man is a given: it is only bad behaviour that requires special pleading), and if as a matter of fact no means exists to cure him, then, while we may with good reason withhold our moral condemnation of him, we might in logic conclude that it were necessary for the good of society to incarcerate him for longer than if he had merely been an erring human being with a normal ability to learn from the consequences of his wrongdoing. There is nothing at all in the appeal to free someone of guilt due to illness that necessitates leniency — quite the reverse in fact.

But in any case it is the sheerest sentimentality to see drug addicts as the victims of an illness.[30] Of course it is true that most such addicts who turn to crime come from unhappy backgrounds; but if it is alleged that these unhappy backgrounds make their addiction inevitable, the same conclusions regarding leniency apply as applied above with regard to illness as a cause of crime.

Most heroin addicts take heroin on and off for a long time before they take it regularly and become physiologically addicted to it. This has been known for a long time. So it is not true that they are 'hooked' by heroin, as they like to say (it is a good principle to examine with care all self-exculpatory claims to helplessness), and it is pure sentimentality to take them at their word. On the contrary, they become addicted to heroin with what can only be called determination, as others become aficionados of wine or postage stamps.

Nor is it true that heroin addiction drives them into criminality with something like the force of destiny. On the contrary: not only has addiction to heroin in the past proved perfectly compatible with regular work and an otherwise law-abiding life, not only are most addicts in contemporary British conditions perfectly well-aware of the life most heroin addicts lead before they ever take heroin themselves, not only does a life of criminality and heroin addiction involve considerable economic efforts that could perfectly well be directed into legal channels, but it is also the case that the great majority of heroin addicts who end up in prison had extensive criminal records before they were ever took heroin. In other words, whatever it was that attracted them to crime probably attracted them to heroin also; and it is pure sentimentality, therefore, to view them as unfortunates driven by pharmacological misfortune to a life of crime.

Now of course not every disagreement pits a sentimental view against a genuinely understanding one. Some people might argue, for example, that it is right to provide heroin addicts with their heroin gratis. They may think this, not because such addicts are ill, or the unfortunate victims of a disease over which they have no control, but simply because, as a matter of empirical fact, to do so causes society less damage than not to do so. Irrespective of whether or not this is correct, it is not a sentimental idea; it relies on no obviously false proposition whose main function is to establish the superior sensibility of the person who makes it.

The seemingly bald statistics on the front page of the newspaper thus depend for their effect on the willing suspension of thought, reflection, questioning and rationality in favour of an immediate emotional response — and this despite the fact that the majority of the newspaper's readers would have been drawn from the most highly-educated segment of society. Sentimentality is confined neither to one situation not to one social class.

The signs manifest themselves in many places. The rear windows of cars, for example, are sometimes festooned with notices to the effect that there is a baby on board, as if the presence of a baby in a car enjoined special care on the part of other drivers in the vicinity. No doubt human beings are programmed by nature to respond solicitously and tenderly to the sight of a baby (although it is clear from history that such programming can be overcome quite easily), but the implication of the notice is that the baby has special rights to be protected from dangerous driving that, say, a thirty-six year old does not have. These notices sometimes even carry a hint of menace: 'Back off — baby on board.' This seems to imply that the driver of the car with the baby might do something violent, or at least aggressive, to you if you do not 'back off.' The transfer of a request for solicitude that is reasonable in some circumstances to a circumstance in which it is not reasonable is thus made the occasion of menace. The sentimentalisation of the baby is accompanied by an aggressive stance to the rest of the world.

Not long ago, a famous footballer, on scoring a goal, removed a baby's dummy that he had been keeping in his shorts for just such an occasion, and stuck it in his mouth in view not only of tens of thousands of spectators in the stadium, but in that of tens and possibly hundreds of millions of television viewers. Apparently, his action was meant to signify to the world that he 'dedicated' his goal to his new-born baby, thereby demonstrating the strength of his love for his baby. The fact that a strapping and athletic young man of twenty-three, engaged in a highly competitive activity not normally known for its finer feeling, should suppose that he was not humiliating himself or making himself ridiculous in the eyes of millions by so infantilising himself, and that he might well have been perfectly realistic in his supposition, suggests that sentimentality is a mass phenomenon almost beyond criticism or even comment.

Demonstrative sentimental public avowals of love of one's children, by means such as tattooing their names on the skin of the arms, are not incompatible with neglect and abandonment of them, of course; indeed, when as a doctor I saw men with the names of their children tattooed on their arms, I could be virtually certain that they were separated from the mother or mothers of their children, and rarely, if ever, saw them. Of course, it is perfectly possible that there are very large numbers of men with the names of their children tattooed on their arms who are extremely good and solicitous fathers, but somehow I rather doubt it; it seems to me more likely that tattooing the name is a substitute for solicitude rather than evidence of it.

The march of sentimentality is now visible even on

our roads and in our cemeteries. The habit of making floral shrines at the site of fatal accidents has grown up quite suddenly (it is always left to others to clear them away when they have withered into a brown mass inside tattered polythene wrappings and constitute just another source of mess in the public domain). I looked at the bouquets at the site of the accident fatal of a teenage driver, and one of the attached cards said, 'Andy, hope you're OK,' which suggests either a residual belief in the afterlife or a rather constricted command of the language.

In about 1990, the inscriptions on the tombstones in our cemeteries suddenly became much more informal than they had hitherto been. Fathers were now, almost without exception, inscribed as dads, mothers as mums; and as family ties weakened, so more of them were mentioned on tombstones. Whereas it was once rarely stated that the deceased was a grandfather or grandmother, now he or she was almost invariably given as a gran, nan, or (in Gloucestershire) granchy. Religious sentiment disappeared at the same time, even from church graveyards; the nearest anyone could come to a religious reflection on the transience of human existence was 'God bless,' a rather thin expression, to put it mildly. (In one such churchyard I found a tombstone with the famous quote from Dylan Thomas, 'Do not go gentle into…' etc., which is not exactly an affirmation, I should have thought, of Christian orthodoxy, or indeed of any faith. A verger told me that the church exercised no control these days over what people put on tombstones.)

It is all as if death itself can, by the employment of informal and sentimental, or even aggressive, language, be reduced to a mere incident of everyday life, and a rather minor one at that; as if the defining condition of the existence of a self-conscious creature such as man, namely his mortality, could somehow be altered, lessened, tamed or domesticated by the employment of diminutives and terms of endearment, or by defiance.

We are now to be sentimental from cradle to grave.

2

What is Sentimentality?

Sentimentality is one of those many qualities that is easier to recognise than to define. The dictionaries, not surprisingly, all point to the same defining characteristics: an excess of emotion that is false, mawkish, and over-valued by comparison with reason. The larger dictionaries — for example, the Oxford English Dictionary — are etymologically, but not psychologically, more detailed than the smaller ones. The OED points out that, originally, the word sentimental had positive connotations: a man who was called sentimental from the middle to the end of the Eighteenth Century would now be called a sensitive and compassionate one, the opposite of a unfeeling philistine brute. The change in connotation was brought about at the beginning of the next century by the romantic-revolutionary poet turned High Tory, Robert

Southey, writing derisively about Rousseau, and was complete by the turn of the Twentieth Century.

The definition above misses an important characteristic of the kind of sentimentality to which I want to draw attention, namely its public character. It is no longer enough to shed an unseen tear in private over the death of Little Nell; it is necessary to do so, or do the modern equivalent, in full public view.

I suspect, though I cannot prove, that in part this is the consequence of living in a world, including a mental world, so thoroughly saturated by the products of the media of mass communication. In such a world, what is done or happens in private is not done or has not happened at all, at least not in the fullest possible sense. It is not real in the sense that reality television is real.

The public expression of sentimentality has important consequences. In the first place, it demands a response from those who witness it. This response has generally to be sympathetic and affirmatory, unless the witness is prepared to risk a confrontation with the sentimental person and be accused of hardness of heart or outright cruelty. There is therefore something coercive or bullying about public displays of sentimentality. Join in, or at least refrain from criticism.

An inflationary pressure also acts upon such displays. There is not much point in doing something in public if, in fact, no one notices it. This means that more and more extravagant displays of emotion become necessary, if they are to compete with others and be remarked upon. Floral tributes grow larger; depth of feeling is measured by size of bouquet. Vehemence and volume of expression are what count.

In the second place, displays of public sentimentality do not coerce only casual passers-by, sucking them, as it were, into a foetid emotional swamp, but when they are sufficiently strong or widespread they begin to affect public policy. As we shall see, sentimentality enables the government to throw sops to the public instead of tackling problems in a determined, rational but also inconveniently controversial way.

But there are those who defend sentimentality. By arguing that there is nothing wrong with it, that on the contrary it is to be applauded, they actually give us a more exact insight into what is wrong with it.

Among the most distinguished defenders of sentimentality was the American philosopher, Robert C. Solomon, who died in 2007. Solomon believed, rightly I think, that emotions were necessary to all cognitive activity and rational thought. Without an emotional stance to the world, after all, one would do nothing, think nothing and seek nothing. A state of complete emotional neutrality would soon lead to death by inanition.

But Solomon went further. In his book *In Defense of Sentimentality*, there is a chapter entitled 'On Kitsch and Sentimentality', in which he attempts to defend sentimentality by rebutting the objections to sentimentality one by one. The objections are six, as follows:

i) That sentimentality involves or provokes the excessive expression of emotion.

ii) That sentimentality manipulates our emotions.

iii) That the emotions expressed in sentimentality are false or faked.

iv) That the emotions expressed in sentimentality are cheap, easy and superficial.

v) That sentimentality is self-indulgent, and gets in the way of proper behaviour and responses.

vi) That sentimentality distorts our perceptions and interferes with rational thought and an adequate understanding of the world.

Solomon then seeks to demonstrate that these objections are false; and in the meantime he tells us that he strongly suspects that those who object to sentimentality are in reality objecting to all emotions whatsoever.

I do not think his suspicion is justified, if for no other reason than that it is extremely difficult — I would say impossible — to conceive of what a conscious life would be like that was entirely emotion-free. It is true that there are some seemingly affectless states in very severe psychiatric illnesses, but most people who suffer from them do in fact express preferences for one thing rather than another, if only by resenting and refusing interference. Even if, for the sake of argument, we grant that these extreme psychiatric states are utterly devoid of emotion, it could not be that anyone would recommend them as a desirable way of life or being, a goal to be reached. Buddhists, it is true, seek to annihilate desire, but mainly because they think that non-existence is preferable to existence, and desiring nothing is a stage in the path to non-existence, at least as an individual consciousness. And very few western philosophers, in any case, are Buddhists.

Thus Solomon's suspicion is that of a straw man set up by himself. The question is not whether there should be emotions, but how, when and to what degree they should be expressed, and what part they should play in human life.

Let us examine, then, his objections to the objections to sentimentality. To the charge that sentimentality provokes (or is in part constituted by) the excessive expression of emotion, Solomon asks 'How much of an emotion is 'too much'? How is this to be measured?'

It is clear that he has suddenly conflated expression of emotion with emotion itself. And it is clear that, in general, we do know what an excessive display of emotion is. Suppose, for example, that I express deep grief over the loss of a pin, weep and wail over it, and remain inconsolable over it for days. Surely most people would find my expression of emotion excessive, not to say bizarre? They would find my behaviour embarrassing or annoying, and would conclude either that I was play-acting, or that I was a person with a highly deformed character, or perhaps that I was psychiatrically ill. They would not, say, ask how much emotion, after all, is too much, how is it to be measured, and so forth. This is carrying scepticism too far.

Of course, different cultures may differ as to how much

emotion ought to be expressed; but I very much doubt whether there is a single one in which the idea of excessive expression of emotion (even if it is only an implicit idea, manifested by social disapproval) does not exist.

And likewise we are all familiar with the idea that some people express too little emotion, for example a parent who loves his child but shows it so little that the child thinks his parent does not love him and does not realise that this is untrue until it is too late. When H.M. Stanley found Dr Livingstone on the shores of Lake Tanganyika, having struggled half across Africa to do so, and lifted his hat uttering the famous words, 'Dr Livingstone, I presume?', the Victorian public found this excessive sangfroid not admirable but laughable. It was carrying self-control, normally considered the mark of a civilised man, to ludicrous lengths.

So there is a universal agreement that the expression of emotion should be consonant both with the emotion itself and with the social situation, even if there is no agreement at what precise point that expression becomes excessive. This in itself should not worry us, or cast doubt on the notion of excessive expression of emotion, any more than the fact that there is no universal agreement over what constitutes a tall man should cast doubt on the existence of tall men.

On the reasonable assumption that it is under conscious control, the degree to which an emotion is expressed is therefore a moral question. What is permissible and even laudable among intimates and confidants is reprehensible between strangers. Indeed, the wish or demand that all emotions should be equally expressible on all occasions and at all times destroys the very possibility of intimacy. If the entire world is your confidant, then no one is. The distinction between the private and the public is abolished, with a consequent shallowing of life.

But it is not only the expression of emotion (that Solomon conflates with emotion itself) that ought to be disciplined: it is the emotion itself that ought to be subject to discipline.

To ask how much emotion is too much — in the expectation that the answer is that we can never say, and therefore that there can never be too much emotion — assumes an almost hydraulic theory. That is to say that a person has a certain amount of emotion that wells up within him (over the quantity of which he has no control), and that, where expression is concerned, it must express itself one way or another — inwardly or much more preferably, according to modern ways of thinking, outwardly (as one man who had just stabbed his girlfriend to death put it to me, 'I had to kill her, doctor, or I don't know what I would've done').

To the extent that men differ biologically by temperament, whether by the operation of genetic inheritance or of some other biological variable, the hydraulic theory contains an element of truth. Some, no doubt, are born phlegmatic while others are born choleric. But the idea that men are, in the matter of the emotions that they feel, simply prisoners of their natural endowments is a very crude and reductive one. The appetite grows with the feeding; and so does emotion with the expression of it.

Anger is a good example of this. A man who loses his temper on the slightest pretext does not grow sweeter-tempered because he expressed his rage so violently the last time. On the contrary, he has a tendency to increase in prickliness, in part because (as everyone who has ever lost his temper knows) there is a certain pleasure to be had from the loss of temper, even if that pleasure is, or ought to be, outweighed by the subsequent remorse it evokes. If a man, on the contrary, controls his temper, and does not express his anger each time he feels it, the chances are that he will soon begin to feel anger less frequently, among other reasons because he will have the time to reflect upon the unimportance of the occasions on which his anger has been so disproportionately aroused in the past. In other words, a man's character is partly of his own making, and what at first requires effort and self-control eventually becomes a disposition.

This being the case, it is not only the expression of emotion, but the emotion itself, that may be excessive. A man who was moved to great anger, however genuine it might be, and whether he expressed it or not, by (shall we say) the arrival of a train at 3.45 and fifteen seconds rather than, as advertised, at 3.45 exactly, would be properly regarded as foolish, if not worse.

Neither emotion nor the expression of emotion is self-justifying, though sometimes they are taken as such, and it is crudely sentimental to suppose that they are. I will give an example of such crudity.

Four authors were asked by the *Guardian* newspaper to discuss the practice of 'outing,' that is to say the public revelation by homosexuals of the homosexuality of other people who wished to keep it concealed and private. Two supported the practice, and two opposed it.

One of the former, Bea Campbell, justified it by arguing that it was an expression of the anger of those people who did it. This anger was entirely free-floating: the writer gave no indication of what the angry people were angry about, let alone whether they were right to be angry about it. And it is hardly surprising in the circumstances, therefore, that she did not answer the question of whether, if they were right to be angry, they were right to express their anger in this particular fashion. The author seemed to have found a Cartesian point of moral epistemology: I'm angry, therefore I'm right.

This is sentimentality, though not of the touchy-weepy variety with which we are more familiar (though perhaps only because we recognise it more easily for what it is than we recognise other varieties).

Solomon refutes the second charge against sentimentality, that it is manipulative, by arguing that all forms of artistic persuasion are manipulative. In point of manipulation, there is nothing to choose (except, perhaps, on aesthetic grounds) between Velazquez's portraits of the dwarves at the Habsburg court of Spain and those cheap pictures of young urchins with tears running down their cheeks. Solomon says that 'we manipulate with our every social gesture,' and therefore no particular form of manipulation is to be preferred, at least from the moral point of view, to any other. On this view, there is nothing to choose — from the point of view of sheer manipulation — between a Nuremberg Rally and a by-election meeting.

Velazquez's portraits of the dwarves manipulate us (if an attempt to make us see something new is manipulation) by showing us the full humanity of our fellow beings whom we might otherwise have been tempted to disregard, despise, write off or ignore completely. Such a reaction is very common. In my practice, for example, I have often noticed how easily people suppose that a person who cannot speak after a stroke cannot understand what is said, and therefore talk about him in front of him as if he were deaf. By painting the dwarves with as much care and commitment as he painted anyone else, by portraying them as highly-intelligent and complex beings exactly like ourselves, Velazquez is drawing them into our moral universe. Once you have contemplated Velazquez's portraits, you will never again be inclined to suppose that the kind of beings that they portray are not morally your equal or worthy of your full consideration as human beings. No longer can you dismiss the subjects of these paintings as funny little creatures whose only function is, intermittently, to amuse you: and if as a result you feel pity for them, it is an educative pity, because so large a part of is incited by your own thoughtless and cruel dismissal of them. It is a pity that requires something of you. And, by causing you to see the humanity of those whom you had previously disregarded as being less than fully human, these pictures cause you to reflect on the very nature of humanity itself.

The pictures of the urchins, by contrast, evoke no such reflections and are not intended to do so. They evoke instead, and are appeals to, a warm and self-congratulatory feeling of sympathy, that assures the person experiencing it that he is a moral person capable of empathising with others, but requires nothing more of him. The comforting and unearned warmth of the feeling is an end in itself, a mere prop to his self-esteem.

When sentimentality becomes a mass public phenomenon, moreover, it becomes manipulative in an aggressive way: it demands of everyone that he join in. A man who refuses to do so, on the grounds that he does not believe that the purported object of sentiment is worthy of demonstrative display, puts himself outside the pale of the virtuous and becomes almost an enemy of the people. His fault is a political one, a refusal to recognise the truth of the old saw, *vox populi, vox dei* — the voice of the people is the voice of God. Sentimentality then becomes coercive, that is to say manipulative in a threatening way.

The third charge against sentimentality, that the emotions it evokes are false or at least self-deceiving, is also denied by Solomon. What, asks Solomon, is a faked emotion? He admits that people can behave as if they had emotions that they do not in fact have, but he says that this is not the case when people are being sentimental. Here I think he is right; and he goes on to say that 'one can even deceive oneself about one's own pretences, and thus fake an emotion in seeming sincerity,' which is also right. But, he says, this is not what is happening when someone is sentimental.

Is it not? The mind, even that part of it that is conscious, is multi-layered, capable of holding different thoughts and feelings in it simultaneously. I learned this as a child when I was accused of something that I knew that I had done, but nevertheless denied having done. My denials could become indignant, and the less they were believed the more indignant I became. A still small voice that actually felt as if it were physically in the rear of my head told me that I was faking it, but I persisted. Reflection told me that my state of mind at the time had been composed of several layers.

I was indignant that anyone could have accused me of a bad deed at all. I was indignant that they could have accused me on a mere suspicion, without full proof, thus reflecting upon what they must have considered my character. I was indignant that they did not believe my denials, thus impugning my veracity. I was upset that I had, in fact, committed a bad deed, thus discovering that I was not an angel. And I was afraid of the consequences of admitting the truth.

In a state of sentimentality, certainly of the sort that is indulged in public, the person is more moved by the fact that he is moved than moved by whatever is supposedly moving him, and furthermore is concerned that everyone should see just how moved he is. The grain of genuine feeling is soon lost in the chaff of secondary considerations; and, exaggeration having a logic of its own, the chaff has a tendency to increase.

The fourth charge against sentimentality is that the emotions involved in it are cheap, easy and superficial. Solomon again finds the charge false. He is uneasy with the word cheap because it sounds snobbish, the opposite being expensive, and the use of it implies for him not a moral or even an aesthetic judgement, but a politico-economic one of an undemocratic nature: that is to say, the people who have cheap emotions are people at the lower end of the socio-economic spectrum.

This suggests that politics — and politics of a certain sort, moreover — ought to be the arbiter of all things. On Solomon's argument, the fact that assault is more commonly committed by members of the lower classes makes it not a crime, or at any rate less of a crime.

In any case, the word 'cheap' is not used in any economic sense, even if sentimental works of art, or reproductions of them, tend to be cheap in money as well as in the emotion they evoke.

Let us compare two literary utterances, one from *Romeo and Juliet*, and one from *Love Story*, by Eric Segal. They are, 'O sweet my mother, cast me not away,' and 'Love is never having to say you're sorry.'

The first, by Juliet, is uttered when, already enamoured of Romeo, her father insists that she marry, and at once, the man of his choosing. If she does not do so he will disown her, or worse. Juliet is appealing to her mother for her support; and, having frequently encountered analogous situations among female patients of Pakistani origin in my medical practice, when girls appealed, usually without success, to their mothers for their support against a marriage that was being forced upon them, I can testify to the precision with which Shakespeare captures in eight words the extreme despair of a girl or young woman in that situation. The mother, until now loved and respected, is her only possible ally; but if she does not support her, she is utterly alone in the world, faced with a choice between repugnance and isolation, with nothing in between.

Let us turn now to the second utterance, of precisely the same length as the first, 'Love is never having to say you're sorry.' What does this actually mean? True enough it imparts a glow to the susceptible, as a sip of whisky imparts warmth to the gullet. But it conveys no truth; if anything, it conveys the opposite of a truth, for love often requires that apologies be made to the one who is loved that in other circumstances might not be offered. The warm glow, then, imparted by these words is unattached to a truth, to a real situation, to a moral dilemma, or indeed to anything else that could be of genuine interest or importance. Cheap, easy and superficial seem quite reasonable words to describe that warm glow.

No doubt we all indulge in sentimentality at times (for it is indeed strange how potent cheap music is), without any great harm coming to anyone as a result. It may even do us some good — a physiologist has suggested that crying with emotion may be a way of ridding the body of excess stress hormones. But what is harmless in private is not necessarily harmless, let along beneficial, in public; and those who think that their private and public behaviour should always be the same, for fear of introducing hypocrisy into it, have a view of human existence that lacks subtlety, irony and above all realism.

The fifth charge against sentimentality is that it is self-indulgent, that it encourages a person to wallow in a warm bath of emotion while supposing himself to be generous in doing so. Sentimentality is self-regarding: it is not just the emotional response to something, (indeed this original emotional response is but only a part of what sentimentality is), but the enjoyment of having the emotion for its own sake. As Milan Kundera puts it:

Kitsch causes two tears to flow in quick succession. The first tear says: how nice to see children running in the grass! The second tear says: How nice to be moved, together with all mankind, by children running on the grass!

But, says Solomon, people such as philosophers enjoy employing reason and logic not just for the truths that doing so may result in, but because doing so is enjoyable in itself and also is a distinguishing mark from others. In a world of individualists, if not of individuals, this is important.

Do we, then, condemn the philosophers as self-indulgent? The answer is yes, if their attachment to (say) the enjoyment of appearing cleverer than the rest of the world is greater than their attachment to truth or wisdom, or so great that they are incapable of changing, if not their minds, at least their utterances. Again, pride may get in the way of seeking truth: we prefer to win an argument by sophistry than to reach the truth by honest inquiry, although the better among us will surreptitiously change out opinions after we have won the day against what we know is right by means of foul play and sophistry.

Of course, there are reasons why we should not give up our beliefs the moment someone produces an argument against them that appears to refute them. Assuming other people to be as sophistical as ourselves, and as intent as we upon winning the argument, they are likely to be no more honest than we. And, unless we are endowed with razor-sharp minds (as most of us are not) that see all the flaws in an argument at once, it is as well to reflect on matters once the element of personal competition and desire for dominance has been eliminated. Too great a readiness to give up beliefs speaks of a lightness of mind, such that nothing is really of importance to it. Changeability can be a sign of frivolity.

The demand that motives be pure is an unreasonable one. Motives are rarely simple, and never pure. The charge against the pleasure of sentimentality is not only that it is self-indulgent, because many, perhaps all, pleasures are at least partly self-indulgent, but that, in its publicly-expressed form, it is dangerously self-indulgent. A sentimental tear shed in private is very different in its consequences from one shed in public, even when the tears involved are only metaphorical.

The final charge against sentimentality cited by Solomon is that it distorts our perceptions and obstructs rational thought and understanding. Sentimentality requires the attachment to a distorted set of beliefs about reality, and also the fiction of innocence and perfection, either actual or potential.

Again Solomon suspects that this is an attack on all emotions for, he says, they are all distorting in one sense or another. In love, for example, one deceives oneself by exaggerating the beauty and virtues of the beloved. It is not merely that, in love, one overlooks certain blemishes, physical or moral; one actually fails to perceive them, or if one perceives them, one rationalises them away until they become imperceptible. Yet no one objects to love on the grounds that it is deceiving. And why, in any case, should we *always* be made aware of flaws and dangers, asks Solomon?

There is both truth and untruth in this. If we were never prepared to overlook anyone's faults we should never achieve friendship, let alone love; and we continue to like or to love despite renewed manifestations of weakness or imperfection in the objects of our liking or loving.

Yet we do not find admirable or joyful any degree of self-deception whatsoever in matters of love. We do not find Eva Braun's adoration of Hitler admirable or even touching; and we pity those among our friends who fall in love with people whom we know to be obviously unworthy of their love and whose manifest and manifold shortcomings will eventually cause our friends great suffering. To elevate romantic love above all other considerations whatsoever can be foolish, to say the least. I did not admire my patient who, on the grounds of such love, returned to a boyfriend after he had had broken her arm and jaw, having not very long before been released from prison after a sentence for killing his previous lover. One may feel sorrow for a woman for whom life with such a man was better than life without him, but not admire her decision to return to him despite all offers of help to escape him, or recommend such a decision to others.

Thus even in private life, the extent to which one is prepared to overlook the shortcomings of others is necessarily a matter of judgement. One can be too harsh or too forgiving, and perhaps people rarely get it exactly right. But the attempt to evade the responsibility of making a judgment at all (which, of course, does not have to be made in conscious, cold-blooded double-entry bookkeeping fashion, like Darwin when he was considering the advantages and disadvantages of marrying) is worse than disastrous.

When emotionality is permitted to spill over into the sphere of public policy, it is not likely that, except occasionally by chance, any good will come of it.

Sentimentality is the expression of emotion without judgment.[31] Perhaps it is worse than that: it is the expression of emotion without an acknowledgement that judgment should enter into how we should react to what we see and hear. It is the manifestation of a desire for the abrogation of an existential condition of human life, namely the need always and never-endingly to exercise judgment. Sentimentality is therefore childish (for it is children who live in such an easily dichotomised world), and reductive of our humanity.

The necessity for judgment implies that our situation in the world, and that of other people, is almost always uncertain and ambiguous, and that the possibility of error can never be escaped. For the sake of a quiet mental life, therefore, we want simplicity, not complexity: the good should be wholly good, the bad wholly bad; the beautiful wholly beautiful and the ugly wholly ugly; the immaculate wholly immaculate and soiled wholly soiled; and so forth.

That is why there is so great an emphasis in the teaching of history in schools nowadays on the Atlantic slave trade and the Holocaust. I do not, of course, wish to deny the very great importance of these two subjects; but their use to sentimentalise the outlook of pupils is evident from the fact that they are taught very little else in history, and are expected to memorise nothing so concrete as a date. The slaves and the people exterminated in the Holocaust can reasonably be presented as nothing but the victims of oppression, and therefore the world can be neatly divided into good and evil.

Again, I do not want to suggest that there is no distinction between good and evil, and nothing to choose between the murderer and his victim. But to insinuate into young minds that human history (and by extension the whole of human life) has been and is nothing but a struggle between victims and perpetrators, oppressed and oppressors, good and evil, is to render them unlikely to develop that sense of proportion without which (as I have put it elsewhere) information is but a higher form of ignorance.

I have already mentioned the schoolgirl who was studying the Rwandan genocide in her history classes, assisted by watching a Hollywood film about it, but this is by no means an isolated case. For many children in our schools, genocidal studies seem to have replaced all other aspects of history whatsoever.

It need hardly be said that genocide is a subject for almost infinite reflection. What, for example, are we to make of the pivotal role of the university-educated elite in the preparation and promotion of the genocide? What does this tell us about the relation between education, culture and morality? What of the responsibility of outside powers, that sit on their hands and fail to intervene, or even deny that they are taking place? At a deeper level, what does the participation of ordinary people, sometimes joyful, sometimes coerced, in the massacre of their erstwhile neighbours and friends, and the appropriation of their goods, tell us about human nature? To what extent do coercion and fear extenuate the vilest actions? What is the relation between the historical explanation of events and their moral evaluation? How do collective and individual responsibility relate to one another?

These are not easy questions to answer. But it is obvious that the only lesson a completely unformed mind can derive from the study — if study it be called — of genocide, in isolation from almost all other knowledge, is of the sentimental four-legs-good, two-legs-bad variety, that the world is composed of good people and bad people; and since most school-leavers will never again study or even think about history, this will be their underlying supposition about all public questions, if not for ever, at least for a long time, a supposition that will leave them susceptible to the siren song of assorted demagogues who claim purity of motive and who tug ruthlessly on heartstrings to attain and retain power. And the pupil comes to believe that, by condemning what is obviously wrong, namely the killing of huge numbers of people, he or she is being virtuous. Public adherence to moral cliché becomes the mark of a good man or woman.

It is time to turn to more examples of sentimentality in action.

3

The Family Impact Statement

In January 12, 2006, a lawyer called Tom ap Rhys Pryce came home quite late from a social function. He was set upon in the street in which he lived by two young men intent upon robbing him. He put up some resistance, but they obtained all that he had on his person that was of use to them: a mobile phone and an underground railway pass. However, they stabbed him many times in the head and chest and he died of his wounds.

The two young men, Donnel Carty and Delano Brown, were caught, tried and convicted of this horrible crime. Before they were sentenced, the prosecutor read out the family impact statement of Adele Eastman, Mr ap Rhys Pryce's fiancée, also a lawyer. She would have liked to read it out to the court herself, but the regulation allowing the close relatives of the victims of murder or manslaughter to do so had not yet quite come into force. The judge therefore gave permission to the prosecutor, presumably to avoid the accusation of unfeeling pedantry.

Ms Eastman said, inter alia:

I had hoped I might be able to read my statement from the witness box in person. I wanted Carty and Brown to hear directly from me the absolute devastation which they have caused.

I must start by saying that my sense of pain and horror at losing Tom, and in such a brutal way, is literally indescribable…

Tom was determined from an early age to reach his full potential in life. He worked incredibly hard and made the most of every opportunity available to him. He gave his best in everything he did and he succeeded. Yet, despite his many achievements, he was the most humble person I have ever known.

In a message left on the tree next to where he died, a friend of ours wrote: 'I remember sitting next to you at our friend's wedding, standing to sing the first hymn, and looking at you as this pure, amazing voice came out. I had no idea, after so many years of knowing you, how beautifully you sang. You were often like that — quietly achieving all these amazing things.'

Tom was my best friend, my soul mate. I adored him — I always will. I miss him more than I could ever describe: his beautiful heart, his brilliant mind, his big loving eyes, his gentle voice, his gleeful laugh and quirky sense of humour, his dancing, our chats and the fun we used to have together. I miss us...

Greed fuelled Carty's and Brown's attack on Tom but it is obvious... that they were trying to play the 'big man.'

I despair at their deeply misguided sense of logic because it is not a man who attacks a defenceless person with a knife, or any other weapon, or hunts victims down in a pack, it is a complete coward, someone who lacks the confidence to take someone on on an equal footing and instead feels the need to put themselves at an unfair advantage.

There can be no sense of victory for Carty and Brown over Tom — he never stood a chance in the first place. He was alone, defenceless and a stranger to violence...

How, on any level, could it have been worth it for them?

Let us now briefly refer to some of the circumstances of the case. The incident was a noisy one. A neighbour, a woman prison officer who, presumably, was no stranger to behaviour that is less than refined, heard the sound of the struggle but, according to reports, was too frightened to look out of her window because there had been two murders that year in the street as well as another stabbing.

The rate of street robbery in that area of London went up from 6.7 per 1,000 inhabitants in 2004 to 10 per 1,000 in 2005.

The two young men were members of a vicious gang that had terrorised the area, and was thought to have committed 90 robberies on the underground in the past two months alone. Three weeks before the murder, Carty and Brown had taken part in robberies on the train in which two men were stabbed. Convictions against the gang were difficult to secure because victims were afraid to testify.

One of the young men had recorded a rap song eight months before the murder. The lyric of the song included the following lines:

I draw for shank [knife]
Your boys will get poked [stabbed] if they come
    round here,
You'll get bored [stabbed] that don't work out that
    draw your sword.
We don't pet [are not afraid] to do murders.

Taxpayers will no doubt be encouraged to learn that this inspiringly tender little song was written and composed while the young man was pursuing a so-called music course at a publicly-funded college.

After they had killed Mr ap Rhys Pryce, the two murderers used his telephone almost at once to call their girlfriends. They also used his underground pass.

I hope I shall not be thought unduly cynical when I say that it seems to me very unlikely that the young men would have been much moved or affected by the victim's impact statement, whether read out by the prosecutor or in person. They surely did not lack the knowledge that their actions would cause distress (or, if they were so strangely constituted that they did lack it, such a statement would not supply the deficiency); it was more that they did not care what distress they caused, or that they gloried in it. The statement would exert no therapeutic influence on them, therefore.

When the fiancée of the murdered man says in her statement that her pain and horror are 'literally indescribable,' we believe her and do not blame her for her inability then to describe it. For most people only the passage of time allows them to put into words what they have experienced, raw emotion often overwhelming the judgment necessary for the true expression or genuine communication of deep distress. What emerge instead is kitsch.

The murdered person, we are told, was an exceptional one. He was talented and charming, yet humble, he sang well and had a beautiful smile. He was clever, had a brilliant future before him, and was going to be married in Italy. His death was a catastrophe for all who knew him. No doubt this is all true; the problem is that, in the circumstances, we dare not mention that it is morally and legally irrelevant. Worse than that, it is actually repugnant, being deeply destructive of law and civilisation.

Would the murder committed by Carty and Brown have been any the less heinous had their victim been a man who did not have a nice smile, who was untalented, who was old and therefore had most of his life behind him, who was socially isolated, who was generally disliked for his many unpleasant qualities, and so on and so forth? (I assume that the murder would have been just as unprovoked.) Is the crime of murder to be reprehended in proportion to the social utility of the victims? This is perilously close to the view of Dennis Nilsen, the serial killer of many young drifting males, who thought society hypocritical for taking so dim a view of his activities. After all, he said, society had cared very little for these people while they were alive; what right had it now, then, to weep crocodile tears over them? The world was not much a worse place without the people whom he killed.

The impression given by the family impact statement is that the crime of murder is heinous because of the particular effects it has on the person making the statement, or on those whom he represents. The corollary of this, of course, is that if the person murdered had no relatives or friends, and was a complete recluse, the killing of him was not much of a crime, for there was no one left to suffer on account of his death. The way would then be open to consider such a killing as laudable, in as much as a socially useless mouth to feed had been eliminated. And are we to conclude that the relatives of murder victims who do not make such an impact statement feel the impact any the less than those who do, that — for example — they feel so ambivalent about the death of their relative that the murderer is a lesser criminal in such cases?

The family impact statement made in court is an open invitation to this kind of irrelevance. A young man was killed in a motor accident by a woman who was subsequently charged with dangerous driving (three children were also killed in the accident). The sister of the young man, in her statement to the court, said:

> Imagine the perfect family... a mum, a dad, a daughter and son. This was the life that I grew up in and was that I had always planned would be the basis of my future...
>
> We both enjoyed swimming... and often went shopping or socialised together.

Again one might ask whether the driver of the car would have been any the less culpable had she happened to hit and kill a man with no sister, who never went swimming, who did not go shopping and did not socialise?

When a Filipino sailor was murdered by a fellow-countryman on board a British ship, his wife had a statement read out in court:

> 'Joel [the murdered person] had a very happy marriage... He was the best and kindest husband and loving father to his children.'

This is genuinely affecting, an infinitely sad and simple statement; but if the murdered man had been estranged from his wife, would his murder have been any the lesser crime?

Family impact statements, not surprisingly, often or usually contain encomia to the victim. What is more alarming is that the police often seem obliged to do so as well. For example, the detective responsible for clearing up the murder of Mr ap Rhys Price said after the convictions of the two young men:

> In murdering Tom ap Rhys Price, Carty and Brown ended the life of a man with so much to live for. A man embarking on a promising career, a man planning his future with the woman he loved, a man supported by a loving family.

This inevitably gives the impression that the police believe that the personal characteristics of the victim are what determines the seriousness of a crime. And this reminds us of the police notices that were put up in the hospital in which I worked, to the effect that anyone assaulting a member of staff in the hospital would henceforth not merely be warned, but prosecuted. In the circumstances, in which there had been many previous complaints by the hospital of police indifference to assaults on staff, this represented progress and something to be grateful for; but the notice did rather give the impression not only that previously assaults had been more or less ignored by the police (something that they had hitherto denied), but that what was important about an assault and made it worth prosecuting was where it took place.

In a sense, of course, an assault that takes place in a public place, perhaps in full view of many other people, and at any rate in front of credible witnesses, on staff who are trying to work for the benefit of all, is rather special in its demonstrative effect. If a man can get away with an assault in such circumstances, it is hardly surprising if people draw the conclusion that they can get away with very much worse when there are fewer witnesses around. But it is still the assault that is the offence, not the brazenness with which it is committed, that is but a symptom of the atmosphere of lawlessness into which we have allowed ourselves, not least through the operation of sentimentality, to decline. An assault on a nurse or a doctor is not worse in itself than an assault on a street cleaner or a tramp.

Even the prosecuting counsel in the case implied in his opening statement to the jury that the murder was especially heinous because of who and what the victim was. He said:

It did not matter to them [the accused] that this man had worked hard for his position in life, that he had a promising career in the legal system ahead of him. It did not matter that he was to marry in September. All that was best in life was ahead of him but to them he was no more than a means to an end and they treated him accordingly.

Of course, the prosecutor was only setting the scene; he wanted to raise the emotional temperature in order to make the jury receptive to his case. Had the victim in fact been a ninety year-old man, or a prostitute, no doubt he would instead have drawn a pathetic picture of the victim's vulnerability, to raise the emotional temperature in the same way; and it is not in human nature that all rhetorical devices should be abjured in a court of law, however much we demand that convictions and acquittals should be based on the evidence presented, and not on mere gusts of emotion. But when the prosecutor, the police and the victim's closest companion all agree that it is the nature of the victim that makes the crime so appalling, we are creating an atmosphere of regression from a regime of laws to one of men. The corollary of the notion that it is peculiarly terrible to kill a man like Mr ap Rhys Price is that it is not so very terrible to kill men who are unlike him.

(On the day after I wrote this, a man, David Martin, was brutally done to death by neighbours when he went round to ask for his son's football which he had kicked into their garden. Among the inevitable pile of flowers marking the scene of the crime was a bouquet with the following inscription: 'Why would anyone do this to you? Did they not know you were too much of a nice person for this to happen to you?' Since what happened to him obviously did happen to him, what the writer must have meant was that Mr Martin was too nice a person to deserve being done to death in this fashion. This implies that there are some people, at least, who merit such a death, whose details I shall spare the reader.)

Let us look at what else Ms Eastman said. Some people might say that it is unfair to subject her statement to detailed criticism because, although most murder trials take place about a year after the crime has been committed, it is only natural that the close relative of anyone who is murdered should be mentally agitated at the time of the trial of the alleged culprit or culprits. Amen to that; but it is precisely in order to try matters according to the facts that courts, at least our courts, are instituted.

Ms Eastman had a degree in Italian and was herself a lawyer. Most murders take place in a somewhat lower part of the social and educational spectrum than hers, and so one might reasonably expect that her family impact statement would be better considered than most. It is not entirely reassuring, therefore, that part of her burden against the convicted young men was that they were cowards, as if, had they given Mr ap Rhys Price a better chance to fight back and prevail over them, what they had done would have been less bad. This implies that to turn our streets into the location of chivalrous jousting — gentleman of Kensal Green, stab first! — would be a step in the right direction.

I do not mean to criticise Ms Eastman personally: I think the defects of what she said are inherent in the whole genre of family impact statement, as it were. And if I were in her position, I would not trust myself to say anything sensible to the court. I would be tempted to go far beyond the kind of things that she said.

It is to avoid understandable excesses of emotion that the law lays down procedures and trials are conducted according to a pre-existing protocol. Why, then, we may ask, have family impact statements suddenly been permitted in British courts?

The official justification, given by the minister who introduced them, Harriet Harman, is that the families of murdered persons often feel excluded from the court proceedings. The family impact statement is intended to change this feeling of exclusion, and replace it, presumably, by one of involvement or participation.

In this justification, we see the elevation of feeling over reason. If the family of the murder victim feels excluded, then this is in itself deemed a sufficient reason to change the procedure. Never mind that, in a civilised society, a court of law is designed to be impartial, and that matters such as verdict and sentencing are supposed to be unswayed by interested parties, which is precisely why they are handed over to judge and jury, and why justice is portrayed as being blindfold. Kangaroo courts and lynch mobs may be influenced by the peculiar virtues of the deceased, but not properly-constituted courts of law.

As it happens, the family impact statements in cases of murder and manslaughter are not permitted to influence the outcome of the case. They are made only after the jury has returned its verdict; and though they are made before sentencing, the judge is specifically enjoined to take no notice of them in the sentence that he hands down. He has to listen, but only as the monkey that hears no evil. Thus only the appearance, not the reality, of the kangaroo court results from such statements.

Pity the poor judge, who listens to an emotional family impact statement, but nevertheless has to hand down a comparatively light sentence immediately afterwards because of important mitigating circumstances, as justice would require. Since most people are at the mercy of the last thing they hear, he will appear to many as an unfeeling brute: how could he so disregard the words of the suffering mother/wife/husband/son/daughter? Injustice will not only have been done, but seen to have been done.

The booklet produced for the families of the victims of murder by the Criminal Justice System, the Home Office, the Crown Prosecution Service and the Department for Constitutional Affairs, and which explains family impact statements, is entitled 'Your choice to have a voice in court.' (Interestingly, the downloaded printed version of the Criminal Justice System's mission statement omits the l, so that the statement reads 'Working together for the public.' I have always suspected that the inefficiency of the system was caused by saboteurs.) Nowhere in the booklet is it explained that the verbal statement will make no difference to anything and will have no practical effect whatever.

The booklet asks, 'What's the point of making a

statement?' The answer is as follows:

> These statements give the families of murder and
> manslaughter victims a voice in the criminal justice
> system. Making a statement enables you to tell the
> court about how the murder or manslaughter has
> affected your family.

And that is all: no mention of the fact that judge may take
no notice of it in his judicial capacity.

Indeed, the opposite impression is given by the old
rhetorical trick of *suggestio falsi* and *suppressio veri*,
suggesting a falsehood and suppressing the truth. The
booklet tells the reader that he can make his statement in
writing, he can have it read out in court by one of the
prosecuting lawyers, or he can read it himself, but that
'However you choose to make your impact statement, the
judge will give it equal consideration.'

Strictly speaking, this is true: for no consideration of
any of them is equal consideration of all of them. But it
is certainly not the impression that the booklet, I suspect
intentionally and with low cunning, gives. The impression
that the family impact statement will make a practical
difference is further strengthened by the following words:

> The family impact statement will be shown to the
> judge, the defence and the prosecution before the
> defendant is sentenced… The court will hear the
> family statement after the defendant is convicted,

but before they (sic) are sentenced.

Who would conclude from this that the family victim statement is, in effect, hot air, that it is mere howling in the wind? For why would a document of no practical importance be made to occupy the time and attention of three highly-paid people if it were, in effect, null and void?

What, then, is the purpose of the family impact statement? On the most generous possible interpretation, it is to give suffering people the opportunity to vent their emotion in public, and thereby, presumably, to reduce their suffering. It is a therapeutic manoeuvre designed to prevent the emotion from turning inwards and causing the sufferer further harm.

This is to make at least two assumptions, the first of which may not be true, and the second of which is certainly not true.

The first assumption is that the venting of emotion in public is always a good and healthy thing, and that the dignified maintenance of silence, or fortitude, is always a bad and unhealthy thing. But even if it were the case that the venting of emotion in public is a good and healthy thing, it does not follow that a court of law is the place to do it.

The second assumption is that a court of law is a therapeutic institution, one of whose objects is to restore psychological equilibrium to victims or to close relatives of victims. In a very loose sense, of course, the courts have a therapeutic function, but for society as a whole, not for the individuals caught up in particular cases: the courts demonstrate that we live in a just, or at least a predictable and therefore not entirely arbitrary, world, where there is redress for wrong impartially administered. If courts offer therapy, it is group, not individual, therapy.

One of the objections to trying the very young killers of Jamie Bulger in a full court of law, with all the intimidating ceremonial attached, was that it was (that is to say, it stands to reason that it must have been) traumatic for them. As it turned out, this was empirically mistaken, as far as can be ascertained, for the two boys turned out well, much better for all the official care and attention given them as the killers of Jamie Bulger. It was a great pity, as the writer Blake Morrison pointed out, that they had to kill Jamie Bulger in order to get a good education, a wholly accurate and justified comment that ought to make every British government minister of the last fifty years hang his head in shame. But children are resilient, and the court ceremonial, besides being much less traumatic than their upbringing at the hands of their relatives, let them know that the world took very seriously what they had done and that it was not a matter to be arranged by a nice cosy chat, in which their feelings were of paramount concern.

The court that tried the boys was not convened to make them feel better about themselves. One might argue about the proper age of criminal responsibility (though the two boys in question knew enough about right and wrong to lie to the policemen who questioned them about their actions); but that is another matter. Criminal courts are not instituted for the psychological benefit of those tried in them, and it is sentimental to suppose that they are.

In any case, it is possible to see something far more cynical and even sinister that lies behind the introduction of family impact statements than a mere mistake about the therapeutic value of venting emotions in public and the proper purpose of the criminal courts. It is no criticism of politicians that they seek factional political advantage from the measures they advocate and institute, but it is a criticism when such advantage is their only real purpose.

There is great unease in Britain about the leniency of the criminal justice system. Almost daily in our newspapers there are stories of violent acts, including murder, committed by those already on bail, or on probation, or recently released from prison early after having served a short sentence for another violent crime.

For example, Garry Newlove went out of his house to stop three young men from damaging parked cars. They set upon him and kicked him to death. One of the three was called Adam Swellings, who had been released on bail only a few hours before he took a leading part in the murder, having been charged with assaulting a young woman and obstructing a police officer. He had been released on bail nine days before that as well, having been charged with assaulting the very same young woman, whose life he had, apparently, made a living hell. It would not have required great powers of clairvoyance to predict that he was unlikely to obey his bail conditions.

In his evidence, Adam Swellings implicitly admitted that Adele Eastman had been right about the way in which street battles ought to be fought. He said, 'It's not right to kick a man on the floor. If anything, you wait until they get back up again to knock them down again.'

Mrs Newlove, now a widow, used the occasion of the conviction of her husband's murderers to draw attention in public to the failures of the criminal justice system. She said that young men in the area had tormented residents. She feared for the safety of her three children if they went to the shops alone. Her car had been damaged many times. At weekends, her family felt imprisoned in their own house by the drunken behaviour outside. A boy had been seriously assaulted outside her house two months before the murder of Mr Newlove. The police had done nothing to deal with the problem. She said, 'It's not acceptable that we always have to wait for fatalities for something to be done... I will fight for Garry and I hope that other families do not have to go through what we have.'

Now it would be grossly sentimental to take a single case such as that of Mr Newlove, however affecting it might be, and however appalling the mistakes made by the criminal justice system, and decide public policy on its basis alone. Any system that deals with a large number of cases must sometimes make mistakes.

An individual case such as that of Mr Newlove, therefore, is illuminating, rather than merely horrifying, only if it is emblematic of something wider than itself; and whether it is emblematic or not requires knowledge and experience to judge. There is internal evidence in the case, however, that suggests that it is.

It would surely require very little knowledge or understanding of human behaviour to realise that a young man on bail for assaulting a girl, who then assaulted the girl a second time, was unlikely to be so impressed by the majesty of the law that he would henceforth obey it merely because he had been asked to do so. The police knew it and the prosecution knew it; it is something that would probably have been appreciated by 99.99 per cent of the country's population. But the magistrate overruled the police and prosecution objections, and let the young man go free, to take drugs and get drunk and murder.

It is possible that the magistrate, in releasing the young man on bail on condition that he should not enter the town where the girl he twice assaulted lived, and where he was soon to murder, was correctly interpreting the guidelines laid down for him by his superiors (judicial decisions are not the reflection of the private opinions or inclinations of judges). But if so, so much the worse for the instructions, which would seem to have little regard for public safety by comparison with some other, entirely secondary, goal, such as keeping the number of young offenders in custody within certain limits, no matter how they behave or what danger they pose.

It might be objected, of course, that if you locked up a hundred or even a thousand such young men, you might prevent only one murder or one serious assault. This seems to me very unlikely, since young men of this nature rarely give up until they meet an immoveable object, or until they mature spontaneously. But even if, for the sake of argument, we accept the above figures, still there would be nothing unjust, quite the reverse in fact, about locking up the hundred or even thousand young men, provided that there were good *prima facie* evidence that they had done what they were accused of having done. And in this case, there was very little doubt about it.

In fact, the number of violent crimes committed by those set at liberty, either on bail or on probation,[32] or released early from prison, having already committed violent crimes, is very considerable. It requires very little reflection also to understand that this way of dealing with violent criminals is organically connected with the rise in witness intimidation, which causes a high percentage of cases brought to court to collapse. If a man is able to say, and say truly, to his victims or other witnesses, 'Remember, I'll be walking the same streets as you in six weeks' time,' it is hardly surprising that the victims or the witnesses are unwilling to testify against him. The result is impunity, at least until the criminal commits a crime that is so grave that it can longer be ignored (*de facto* if not *de jure*). In such circumstances, the criminal may admit his guilt, in words such as 'I was bang out of order,' suggesting that, up to the time he committed the crime that could not be ignored, he was perfectly in order. You can maim and terrify, but you cannot kill.

In other words, although Mrs Newlove was drawing wide conclusions from a single case, that of her husband, she was not being sentimental in doing so, indeed she was attempting to perform a public service by enunciating an argument. She was impelled, no doubt, by anger — but who would not be angry in her circumstances? However, the expression of her anger and other emotions was not an end in itself, as it is in the family impact statement. If it was therapeutic for her, this was not its purpose.

It is evident that the family impact statement is (or at least could reasonably be interpreted as) an elaborate ruse to mislead the families of murdered people, and the public, into thinking that the criminal justice system and the government is sensitive to their concerns about the high levels of violence in society. It would hardly be going too far to say that the family impact statement is designed (in effect, if not in purpose) to reduce the likelihood of people like Mrs Newlove from complaining to the media by satisfying them with their day in court, under the delusion that they are making a difference.

Such a ruse could work, of course, only in a society in which it was largely accepted that the expression of emotion was a good in itself, independent of whatever other effect it might have: a society thoroughly sentimentalised.

4

The Demand for Public Emotion

On May 3, 2007, a little girl called Madeleine McCann went missing at the beach resort of Praia da Luz in the Algarve in Portugal. Her parents, both doctors, were dining about a hundred and fifty yards away, having left her and her younger twin siblings in their holiday flat, returning to check on them every half hour or so. At about ten o'clock, Madeleine disappeared, as yet no one knows how or with whom. The case caught the imagination, or at any rate the media attention, of the whole world, and before long Maddy's face was as recognisable as that of any movie star or footballer.

It helped that she was an attractive child with a very winning smile. She was childhood innocence personified; her parents, educated and successful, were precisely the type to whom tragedies of this type did not normally occur, but who progress through life like a hot knife through butter, earning a lot of money and retiring without financial anxiety in their old age. For this reason, no doubt, they were able to mobilise the media of mass communication, which were as ever alert to the possibilities of the story. Sales of newspapers in Britain rose significantly in the first days of the drama, and in the subsequent months the case cast a lurid light upon the emotional life not just of Britain, but of many countries. The disappearance of Madeleine, and the attempts of her parents to find her, provoked displays of emotion that were astonishing, considering that the McCanns were completely unknown to them.

A single case, well chosen, can be emblematic or illustrative of a wider problem, of course. Seventy-seven thousand children went missing in Britain last year, and while the vast majority of them were found or returned within hours or days, a significant number of them became what the police call 'long-term missing,' the continued absence of each of whom presumably caused immense anguish to someone. But I have never seen the case described in the wider context of children who have disappeared. The particular in this instance has remained strictly particular. In all probability, the very attractiveness of the child herself, and the fact that the parents were themselves happy, attractive and successful professionals of the kind whose children do not generally go missing in murky circumstances, assisted in turning the disappearance into a *cause célèbre*, partaking equally of the characteristics of a murder mystery and a Hollywood premiere.

By no means all the emotions evoked by the case have been tender; indeed, sometimes they seem to be simultaneously tender and brutal, as when a black woman called Shona Adams, who runs a model agency specialising in finding the doubles of celebrities, received death threats and racial abuse after it became known that she had found a young girl who so resembled the missing Madeleine that she might be contracted for a huge sum of money to play the role of Madeleine in a film to be made of the whole episode, of which, of course, the agency would get a generous share. (Apparently, the agency had received approaches from a hundred would-be doubles, or rather, from the parents of such doubles.)

What can have been going through the minds of those who threatened Shona Adams with murder? By acting in this way they presumably thought of themselves as guardians of Madeleine's flame, whatever that might be; perhaps they thought of her memory as being too precious to be sullied and exploited in so crassly commercial a fashion. But if this was so, it is surely rather odd that the owner of the agency alone should have been selected to receive death threats, since she was not the only link in a chain of commerce. Moreover, and more fundamentally, it is difficult to see how threats of violence, whether sincerely meant or not, could serve to keep Madeleine's memory unsullied by worldly considerations.

What kind of sentiment is it that impels a person to threaten to kill a complete stranger because of her involvement in the commercial exploitation of the disappearance of another complete stranger, albeit one not yet old enough to have yet committed the sins of the average human being? Almost certainly the sentiment is intense but shallow and fleeting, to be resurrected in the near future by another heart-rending, tear-jerking case. And once again sentimentality seems to be dialectically related to violence and brutality, in imagination if not in deed.

Another non-tender act elicited by the case was an electronic petition sent to 10 Downing Street. It read as follows:

We the undersigned petition the Prime Minister to request that Leicestershire Social Services fulfil their statutory obligation to investigate the circumstances which led to 3 year old Madeleine McCann and her younger siblings being left unattended in an unlocked, ground floor hotel room. We ask that the Prime Minister do this to reflect an even-handed approach to the important issue of child protection. We also wish to ensure that no parent will ever be able to evade responsibility for the safety and welfare of their children by citing the example of Mr and Mrs McCann, whose negligence is unreasonably being discounted in the tidal wave of sympathy brought about as a consequence of their media campaign.

This beautiful document was one of 29,000 petitions received by 10 Downing Street since it started its electronic petition scheme about a year ago, though the petition was rejected, as thousands of others were, on the grounds of its offensive language. (The whole scheme is in any case suspect, another sop to a public increasingly aware that the government machine has escaped its control entirely. And, not surprisingly, it is an invitation to sentimentality. 'We the undersigned petition the Prime Minister to speak to the European Union or anyone in power to press about Bulgaria's abandoned children.' Why specifically Bulgaria's abandoned children, one cannot but ask? And what is it to 'press about' something, as if showing one's concern were an end and virtue in itself?)

Doubts about the wisdom of the manner in which the McCanns left their children while they dined at a restaurant a hundred and fifty yards away must have occurred to many people, above all to the McCanns themselves, but it surely takes a special kind of nastiness, a sadism masquerading as a sentimental concern for the safety of children, to start a petition asking for them to be punished further than by the loss of their child — unless, that is, you believed that they were directly responsible themselves for Madeleine's disappearance.

But the McCanns appealed to the sentimentality of the world in a manner that might be called unscrupulous. On a website visited by 80 million people in the first three months after Madeleine's disappearance, there was the opportunity to buy merchandise, including Look for Madeleine wristbands, described as 'good quality… to keep reminding you about Madeleine,' with poster included, and T-shirts with a picture of Madeleine on them, with the legend 'Don't You Forget Me' inscribed on it.

I confess that a parallel with the sentimental merchandising of Che Guevara's image came to my mind. I found the words 'Don't you forget me' disturbing, and very different in meaning from 'Don't forget me.' The latter is an appeal, the former is bullying or menacing in tone. Don't you forget about me, it seems to say, or else. But what is this 'or else'? A kind of curse? If you forget me, some terrible misfortune will befall you? More likely, if you forget me you will have no right to consider yourself or be considered by others a decent, compassionate person: and this despite the fact that, however much you remember Madeleine, it is in the last degree improbable that you will in any way be able to assist in finding her. We are here in the realm of King Berenger I, the protagonist of Eugene Ionesco's play, *Le Roi se meurt* (Exit the King), in which the king, utterly self-centred and egotistical, makes the following speech of existential despair when he learns that he is soon to die and cannot escape his death:

> Let them remember me. Let them cry, let them despair. Let them perpetuate my memory in all the history textbooks. Let everyone know my life by heart. Let all the schoolchildren and all the scholars have no other subject of study but me, my kingdom, my exploits. Let them burn all other books, let them destroy all other statues, let them put mine in all public places. My picture in every ministry, in every town hall, in the tax offices, in the hospitals. Let them give my name to all the aeroplanes, all the ships. Let all the other kings, soldiers, poets, tenors, philosophers be forgotten and let there be nothing but me in everyone's mind. One first name only, one surname for everyone. Let children learn to read in spelling my name: B – e – Be, Berenger. Let me be on the icons, on millions of crosses in all the churches. Let them say masses for me, let me be the Host. Let the rivers outline my profile in the plains. Let them call to me eternally, let them supplicate to me, let them implore me.

Again, it is difficult to see how the wearing of a wristband inscribed with Madeleine's name could be of practical use in finding her. (I noticed that the small and large sizes had sold out, but I do not know how many were offered for sale in the first place. I assume it was many thousands.) Their main function was to raise money for the company that the McCanns set up in the aftermath of Madeleine's disappearance, a company that was not a charity, as many people must carelessly if understandably have supposed, but a not-for-profit company among whose aims was the financial support of the McCann family (i.e. themselves) as they went round the world in search of — well, in search of what, exactly? Their daughter? Absolution? Publicity?

Their frenzy of activity, understandable in the circumstances though not necessarily laudable, would have had no effect if the world had not been prepared to pay attention to them. The media knows a story that will appeal to mass-sentimentality when it sees one, and thus created a market for Madeleine wrist-bands.

What could have been in the minds of those who purchased them? Perhaps they thought that they were performing an act of charity in doing so, but it is possible to contribute to charity without demonstrating that you have done so: indeed, the traditional religious teaching in the west is that we ought to perform our acts of charity away from the gaze of others.

Moreover, a moment's thought is sufficient to establish that every person who had heard of the disappearance of Madeleine, except for those who were responsible for it and for a few people of malevolent disposition, would hope that she were soon returned safe and sound to her parents. They would not hope this very deeply, of course, because they would have many other things, much more important to them, to worry about; but in so far as the case entered their consciousness at all, they would hope that Madeleine had not been done to death.

For those who bought the armbands, or for that matter the T-shirts, this tepid reaction to the tragedy would not be sufficient. To be a virtuous person one must feel every tragedy as one's own. This could place rather a strain on people, there being so many tragedies in the world; but fortunately, only a few of them ever come fully to light. And when a tragedy such as Madeleine's does come to light, one has the duty to react to it as if it affected one personally.

The purchaser of the armband is demonstrating to the world the strength of his compassion and therefore of his virtue; and furthermore, he is demonstrating the superiority of the strength of his compassion and therefore of his virtue, by comparison with those — always likely to remain in the majority — who did not buy an armband. He is thus of an elite, emotional and moral. Never was there better value for money (the armbands, high quality, were two pounds each).

The interest aroused by the case was worldwide: and there were soon more sightings of Madeleine, from Morocco to Belgium, than of the Loch Ness monster in all its history. When the McCanns went to Morocco to follow up on a sighting there, they visited a primary school there, as if they were heads of state, whose children had produced a number of posters asking for the return of Madeleine. They had an audience with the Pope, who offered his prayers to the efforts to find their daughter, and Vanity Fair ran a long article about the case. A feature film was mooted, and American television stations were said to be in a bidding war to interview the McCanns.

If sentimentality comes, can nasty-mindedness be far behind? The chief feature writer of the *Sun*, Oliver Harvey, saw fit implicitly to accuse the McCanns of killing their own child, the evidence for which was that they had displayed insufficient emotion in the days following the disappearance. The newspaper had previously asked its readers to help find Madeleine by wearing a yellow ribbon, without of course explaining what the connection between the two might be (sentiment being so much more important than reason); but Mr Harvey, fighting back his natural inclination to sympathise with the grieving parents, had this to say:

My misgivings began with the lack of emotion shown by the McCanns in those first few days after Madeleine went missing. No streaming tears, no trembling lips, no sobs of despair. Now the unease has become an awful gnawing doubt. It hurts me to say this, but now I fear something is amiss with Kate and Gerry's [the McCanns'] story. So is it possible the McCanns could bury their own daughter in secret and concoct a big fiction to fool the world? One theory... is this: Madeleine is given too much sedative to help her sleep. She dies, by accident. The McCanns have to make a snap decision to save their careers and stop the twins being put in care or place themselves with a foreign judiciary.

In other words, because the McCanns did not cry or sob in front of the cameras, as the multitudes have a right to expect and demand, as if the world were a giant gladiatorial amphitheatre for their amusement, it follows that they accidentally killed their own child and buried her to save their careers. This monstrous inference, published for several millions to read, is based upon the assumption that those who do not weep do not feel, and that those who do not feel must be guilty of the most heinous crimes.

It is not as if the writer of these odious lines is wholly reliable as to the nature of his own feelings. When he tells us that the unease has become 'an awful gnawing doubt', you wonder. Awful gnawing doubts, indeed! If he really thought the doubts were awful, if they truly gnawed, he would keep them to himself, because a doubt by its very nature means that what is doubted is not certain. Not being sure that what the McCanns say is true entails not being sure that what they say is false. And if what they say is true, then to the pain of having lost a beloved child the writer of those lines has heaped upon them the pain of a public accusation of murder, a truly vile thing to do. Things that may permissibly be thought and said in private may not permissibly be thought and said in public; but of course, the dissolution of the distinction between the two realms, private and public, is one of the aims of the sentimentalist.

Oliver Harvey was not the only one to find evidence of guilt in the Mrs McCann's self-control. Amanda Platell wrote that she hadn't seen 'such creepy control in a woman since Linda Chamberlain cried "My God, the dingo's got my baby."' In other words, self-control equalled guilt; guilt by association could not be more clearly implied.[33]

Now of course it is perfectly true that people who have committed the most dreadful acts may sometimes show no emotion afterwards, either because they are, by character, without normal human feelings, or because they have, by some psychological method or other, obstructed the memory of what they have done from reaching their consciousness. About a third of murderers cannot remember what they have done, and some psychophysiologists have proposed a physiological explanation of why this should be so. According to these psychophysiologists, Tolstoy was wrong when he wrote that murderers who said that they did not remember their deeds were simply lying; be that as it may, it is not easy to express emotion about what you cannot remember, or even what you falsely claim not to be able to remember. For to display much emotion in the latter circumstances would be to give the game away.

But if it is true that some people who are guilty display no emotion, it does not by any means follow that all people who display no emotion are guilty, or that all those who do display emotion are innocent. In my career as a prison doctor, I soon learnt what in any case should have been obvious from mere reflection on human nature, which is to say that I should not take the emotional expression of those on remand and who were awaiting trial as evidence in itself of either guilt or innocence. There is, perhaps, a natural propensity to do so, but it should be resisted. Though by no means especially naïve, I recall one man whose protestations of innocence over a brutal murder with which he was charged were so consistent and so convincing that I thought he must indeed be innocent. As soon as he was found guilty, however, and returned to the prison from court, he described his actions in the most horrifying and graphic detail. And surely it is by now a commonplace that the relatives of murder victims, who appeal tearfully on television for witnesses to the crime, sometimes turn out themselves to be the murderers.

It emerged that the McCanns had been advised not to display emotion in public, because (it was said) Madeleine's abductor might derive pleasure from seeing their distress. But this did not prevent either the newspapers or the bloggers from referring to their lack of emotion, which in their opinion should have been simply too strong to control. One blogger wrote:

I'm not saying that she [Mrs McCann] is responsible for her [Madeleine's] disappearance or death, but one thing has struck me from the very beginning when Madeleine first disappeared, was the total lack of emotion by both the McCanns. In my recollection over the years of seeing mothers on TV whose child has just gone missing is extreme emotion! distraught!... to say the least! Mrs McCann in particular has always struck me as being 'poker faced' or 'steely faced' for a mother that cannot find her child... completely the opposite to what I have seen in the past, or what I would have expected.

The disclaimer at the beginning of this entry is simply not credible; for if Mrs McCann's alleged poker-face is not evidence of her guilt, or at least collusion, what could be the point of mentioning it? It seems that the refusal of the McCanns to exhibit their emotions in public caused so much hostility towards them, and so much abuse, that the *Daily Mirror* felt constrained to close down its website devoted to the case.

One or two newspapers tried to salvage the public reputation of the McCanns by reporting that they did sometimes show their emotions publicly. *The Times*, for example, reported that Mrs McCann had cried in the aeroplane on her way back from Portugal to England, while the *Daily Mirror* reported that she cried when she returned, alone, to Madeleine's pink-painted bedroom. (How alone could she have been for it to have been reported, unless, of course, the whole thing was made up?) If you want public sympathy, it seems, you must cry in public; grieving is like justice, it must not only be done, but be seen to be done. And God help those who do not cry.

The demand that emotion should be shown in public, or be assumed not to exist and therefore indicate a guilty mind, is now not an uncommon one.

A young British woman called Joanne Lees was driving through the centre of Australia with her boyfriend, Peter Falconio, in 2001, when they were stopped by a man on the pretext that there was something wrong with the vehicle in which they were driving. The man shot Peter Falconio, and then tied up Joanne Lees, almost certainly preparatory to raping and killing her. However, she managed to escape and run into the bush, where the assailant could not find her.

She told her story when she reached safety, but since the body of her boyfriend was never found, it met with some scepticism. What is more, her lack of emotion in front of the reporters and television cameras led many to suspect, and even to accuse, her of either making the whole story up, or, even worse, of being herself a murderess. For a time, the police seemed to suspect her. Emotional restraint was once again taken as evidence of lack of emotion and therefore of a guilty mind.

More than four years later, a man called Bradley John Murdoch, a man with a long history of criminality, was found guilty of the murder and attempted abduction. He was sentenced to serve twenty-eight years in prison, and his appeal against conviction was dismissed. Joanne Lees had been entirely vindicated, at least officially.

However, even after Murdoch's conviction, an Australian broadcasting station, Network Nine, saw fit to hold a poll to discover if Australians thought that the convicted man was guilty. The cruelty of this to the victim of so horrible a crime hardly needs pointing out (and even if Murdoch were innocent, even if, against the odds, there had been a miscarriage of justice, a poll in his favour would not have constituted worthwhile evidence).

Almost the only reason that the poll could be carried out was that public sympathy for the victim was never very great. And *The Australian* made the reason for this clear:

Joanne Lees has never enjoyed great sympathy from the public, both here and in the UK, perhaps because of the lack of emotion she showed in public after the 2001 abduction and murder.

The *Daily Mail* in Britain made a similar point:

Miss Lees' apparent lack of emotion after Mr Falconio's death led many to question her story...

A few days after Peter Falconio's disappearance, an article in the *Guardian* pointed out, though not with approval, that if Joanne Lees had burst into tears in public, or made emotional appeals in front of the cameras for witnesses, then (notwithstanding the fact that those who make such appeals do indeed sometimes turn out to be the culprit in the case) she would have been more readily believed.

After Murdoch's conviction, Joanne Lees was criticised for 'cashing in' on her experiences, for having given interviews for which she was paid a great deal of money, for having accepted a large advance for a book, and for considering a film version of her story. One might have supposed from this reaction that we lived in an ascetic society of anchorites utterly indifferent to material wealth. Her book, that of a very ordinary young woman without literary talent (or pretensions), was in its own way symptomatic of modern emotional shallowness, for it is filled with every possible cliché of psychobabble, from people always being there for her to the need just to be herself. Psychobabble is, of course, the means by which people talk about themselves without revealing anything, and certainly without having undergone the painful process of genuine self-examination. It is, in effect, the public manifestation of self-obsession without any commitment to truth. But still her refusal to bow to pressure to be emotional in public did her a great deal of credit.

What does this pressure signify? In the first place, the abandonment of a cardinal virtue, fortitude, as a cultural ideal. To control the expression of one's emotions in order not to inconvenience or embarrass others, and for the sake of one's own self-respect, is now seen as being far from admirable. On the contrary, it is seen as psychologically damaging to oneself and as treachery to others.

It is psychologically damaging to oneself because repression inevitably results in harmful effects later on: for emotion is a fluid that, like all fluids, cannot be compressed, and therefore will make itself manifest in one way or another. For example, those who do not grieve properly for a lost loved one, which is to say who do not express themselves by sobs and tears and wailing, will become seriously depressed a little later in their lives; while those who do not express their anger are more likely to suffer heart attacks or contract cancer. Unexpressed aggression towards others inevitably turns into aggression towards oneself.

Concealing one's emotions is treachery towards others because it implies mistrust of them, and lack of confidence in their capacity for compassion. Concealment is furtive, secretive, dishonest and guilty; while the good man has nothing to hide and lives his life completely in the open. Indeed, the better he is, the more open he is: ideally, we should live in a completely stream of consciousness world in which we say unreservedly all that we think. And since, when we are abducted and threatened with murder in the Australian outback, it is only natural that we should be very distressed, it follows that someone who claims that she has had such an experience but shows little emotion about it must either be lying or be a bad, secretive, furtive, dishonest, mistrustful person unworthy of our sympathy.

The demand that life be lived openly in this fashion is an impossible one. Most of us would probably be lynched within minutes if we decided to express in public every thought that came into our minds. But just because a demand or an ideal is impossible to put into practice, it does not mean that it has no influence or importance. The expectation that people express their emotions, on pain of being believed to have none, actually inhibits the exercise of imagination, and a faculty that is not used soon withers. Why make an effort to imagine if everything is supposed to be explicit? But since life cannot be lived with everything made explicit, it means that our sympathy for and empathy with other people declines rather than increases with the expression of emotion, at least when it becomes too routine and extravagant. A man who exclaims 'Damn!' once in his life conveys more by it that a man who employs far more vulgar expressions continually. Like all currencies, that of emotional expression can be inflated and debased; and again, as with currency, the bad drives out the good.

The expectation, rising to the shrill demand, that people express their emotions in public after a traumatic experience is essentially tyrannical. It fails to recognise that people are by nature different from one another; according to the demand, everyone must conform to a single standard of conduct or risk being thought inhuman, stuck-up or hoity-toity (an expression frequently used of Jeffrey Archer's wife because of her stoical and undemonstrative support of him throughout his various disreputable exploits).

The case of Joanne Lees was not the first in Australia in which lack of emotion was taken as evidence of the guilt of the person who showed it. In 1980, a baby called Azaria Chamberlain disappeared in the bush of the Northern Territory, near Ayer's Rock. The mother, Linda Chamberlain, reported the disappearance to the police, saying that she thought a dingo must have taken the baby. There was considerable controversy as to whether dingoes could or ever did behave in this fashion; it has now been as conclusively proved as any fact of animal behaviour can ever be proved that they can and do.

Not surprisingly, the case aroused a great deal of interest (to put it mildly) in the press and on television. At first, Linda Chamberlain's story was believed; but public opinion turned decisively against her when she appeared cold and unemotional. She did not break down in public and weep, as the occasion seemed to demand, and as many people assumed she would have done had her loss not been self-inflicted. In this atmosphere, she was convicted of murder and sentenced to life imprisonment.

A few years later, evidence was found that exonerated her, and corroborated her original account of the disappearance. It is now generally accepted that a dingo did take Azaria Chamberlain. The mother's lack of emotion at the time, therefore, was caused by conscious self-restraint and a desire to uphold her dignity rather than guilt; but self-restraint and dignity are now themselves a form of treachery, that is to say a treachery towards the emotions.

In the wake of the death of Princess Diana, the Queen did not openly display any grief at the loss of her former daughter-in-law. The fact that this absence of display of emotion was universally taken as a public relations disaster for the Royal Family was itself highly significant, for it suggested that it is the public nature of the expression of emotion that is most important. Emotions are now like justice: they must not only be felt, but seen to be felt.

The tabloid newspapers carried out what can only be called a campaign of bullying against the sovereign. They demanded that, against custom and usage, the Union flag be flown at half-mast over Buckingham Palace, for what is a mere tradition to be set against a gust of popular emotion? To argue that a tradition should take precedence over such a gust in determining such a matter as whether or not a flag be flown is akin to heresy: for it suggests that the wishes of we, the people, should not be sovereign at all times and at all moments, that *vox populi* is not necessarily and in all circumstances *vox dei*. And this is anathema to the political philosophy that, consciously or not, has now taken possession of most men's minds. It does not worry them that, if they feel no obligation to the customs, traditions and achievements of those who came before them, their own successors will feel no obligation to their customs, traditions and achievements. *Now, this very instant* is the only moment in history that counts.

'Where is our flag?' asked a newspaper headline, and 'Show us you care' shouted the crowd outside Buckingham Palace (perhaps by laying a teddy bear on one of the piles of stuffed toys that had already accumulated in impromptu shrines around the country). To this pressure, the Queen eventually gave in, though with a subtlety that outwitted the emotional bullies and blackmailers.

The bullies knowingly or unknowingly overlooked several aspects of their own behaviour, leaving to one side the fact that in a constitutional monarchy the relationship of the monarch to the people is not that of elected representative, let alone that of provider to customer. The fact that the monarch was by then quite advanced in years was of no account to them; for in a society in whose culture youth is not only the fount of all wisdom and the touchstone of worth, but is treated both as an aspiration and an achievement, no respect is due to age, nor any effort made to enter into the worldview of someone born in a different age.

Indeed, the bullying of the monarch was symptomatic of an intolerance of any reaction to the death of the princess other than their own. At a time when diversity of culture was supposedly valued for its own sake, certain cultural differences were not to be tolerated or even permitted. The Prime Minister of the time, a man who made much of his own youthfulness, which he appeared to suppose, and certainly wished, to last forever, Mr Blair, caught the mood of the emotional bullies perfectly: the deceased was 'the People's Princess.' Thereafter, even to express mild doubts as to the conduct or achievements of the Princess required a certain courage, for to do so was to be, by implication, an enemy of the people. The judgement of the majority, or at least of those people who made the most fuss, must be right: forty million teddy bears can't be wrong.

'Show us you care,' shouted the crowds outside the palace, without the self-knowledge that they were bullying rather than expressing any genuine grief. Now, either the Queen felt grief at the death of her former daughter-in-law, or she did not; if she did, she was surely within her rights to grieve privately. She was brought up at a time when it was considered a matter of decency for people not to expose their emotions very strongly in public, rather than culturally absurd and psychologically damaging; moreover, as constitutional monarch, it was her duty to swallow her emotions whenever she appeared in public, often with people whom she must have detested or despised. Such self-control, dutifully exercised over more than half a century, must have become second nature to her. For very good reasons, she was not the kind of person given to emotional self-display.

Of course, it is perfectly possible that she felt no, or very little, grief. Not even the most ferocious critics of the Princess, however, would have considered it right for the Queen at that moment to rehearse in public her reasons for not feeling any grief, even if they were very good and sufficient ones. Indeed, it would have been very wrong for her to have done so. But if, in fact, she did not grieve for her ex-daughter-in-law, then the demand by the mob that she display grief was in effect a demand that she lie to it, that she play-act for its delectation.

Besides, there is something distinctly peculiar about the demand that she should show that she cared. It was a curiously open-ended demand. Cared about what or for whom? It was not specified. That she cared for her ex-daughter-in-law? For the causes the dead Princess promoted? For the mob itself? It really did not matter much, so long as she expressed emotion of some sort, at the behest of the multitude. It was a demand that she conform.

The public expression of deep emotion, or supposedly deep emotion, is intrinsically coercive. This is not to say that it is never appropriate, only to say that the question of appropriateness arises. When someone expresses a powerful emotion, or when a rather less powerful emotion is expressed en masse, some kind of participation or reaction by an on-looker is expected. This is only to be expected. We normally attempt to console someone whom we judge to have good reason for his manifest grief; we congratulate someone who is joyful on the reception of excellent news. The closer our relation to or with the person who expresses the strong emotion, the closer to his emotion our own reaction generally is, though there are exceptional circumstances in which this might not be so, for example in the immediate aftermath of disasters. If we stand stonily by a person in a state of high emotion that we properly judge to be genuine, and evince absolutely no sign of having been moved by it, we are suspected of heartlessness.

Moreover, we all accept that there are outward forms with which we should comply. If you see a funeral procession go by, you do not indulge in hilarity at that moment, even if you are feeling unusually joyful, at that precise moment, though the person whose funeral it is may be completely unknown to you. It is not that you feel particular sorrow for the deceased — how could you, not knowing who he was? — but there ought to be in our comportment in the circumstances a decent recognition of the ultimate fate of us all, in our common humanity, and a respect for the feelings of the mourners. But while you might stand still for a moment, be silent and even hang your head slightly, to shed tears would be grossly histrionic.

So the appropriate response to the emotions of others depends upon a number of factors. What is clear, however, is that the proper ordering of responses depends for its possibility upon the general honesty of emotional expression, that is to say on the absence of hysteria or a desire to express more than what is felt. We would be compassionate with a man who remained for years inconsolable over the loss of a bottle top, not as a man who was grieving, but as a lunatic.

The demand that the Queen show the crowd that she cared, as the crowd claimed itself to care, whether in fact she did or didn't share their supposed emotion, subverts the whole notion of honesty and proportion of expression. A demand to show respect in outward form is one thing; a demand to express an inward state another. The crowd was in effect demanding that the Queen lie to it, or at any rate be prepared to do so; and the question arises as to what kind of people demand to be lied to in this fashion. The answer, bullies and tyrants. It wasn't so much what she said in response to their bullying that counted as a triumph, therefore, but that she was forced to say anything at all, and thereby abandon her own code and accept the crowd's.

She was not the only one to experience the venom of the sentimentalists after the death of the princess. When Professor Anthony O'Hear published a relatively mild article, suggesting that the princess had displayed 'childlike self-centredness' throughout her adult life, and that the public mourning after her death was symptomatic of 'a culture of sentimentality,' some of the tabloids reacted with fury, one of them calling him a 'poisonous professor, a rat-faced, little loser,' not exactly a powerful argument, but a powerful illustration how quickly sentimentality turns to menacing vituperation or worse. It served as a warning to others of like mind not to express their views in public.

It was this tendency to vituperation, with its undercurrent of incitement to violence, that prevented the many people who did not regard the death as an important national tragedy from expressing their views for quite a long time. They laid low until it was safe to speak, until the storm of sentimentality had safely passed. When finally those voices were raised in public, they received more support than insult.

Those critics who say that the episode of the princess's death and its aftermath was not of cultural significance because the majority of the population did not take part in the histrionic public scenes (strangely enough, no surveys of attitudes or reactions to the death were taken immediately after it) are missing the point. Even if it was only a small minority that went in for extravagant demonstrations of grief-like behaviour, it was a minority that was able to impose its tone, at least for a time, on the whole country. To dissent was to be an enemy of the people.

Of course, the struggle between the explicit and the implicit expression of emotion, between the crude and the refined, between the false and the true, the hysterical and the honest, is not entirely new, at least if we can take Shakespeare's word for it. Coriolanus sought the people's vote in order to be tribune, and was advised to show his war wounds to the crowd (or rather mob, for all crowds in Shakespeare are mobs) in order to gain its favour. Coriolanus is too proud to do so; he thinks his signal services to the state should speak for themselves, without any such vulgar display.

> What must I say?
>   'I pray, sir?' — Plague upon it, I cannot bring
> My tongue to such a place. 'Look, sir — my
>   wounds.
> I got them in my country's service when
>   Some certain of your brethren roar'd and ran
> From the noise of our own drums.'

Of Coriolanus's refusal to show his wounds to the crowd (to show that he cared), the Second Citizen says:

> Not one amongst us... but says
>   He us'd us scornfully; he should have show'd
> us
> His marks of merit, show'd us wounds received
>   for's country.

It is Coriolanus's tragedy that, through his excessive pride of caste which he mistakes for honour, he actively provokes the hostility of the mob (there would be no tragedy at all if he were an immaculate hero with no blemishes in his character). But if Coriolanus contributes very largely to his own downfall, there can be no doubt what Shakespeare thinks of the mob and its demands — indeed, Shakespeare's depiction of mobs in general is a rare clue to his own personal views.

At any rate, Coriolanus's position was very different from that of the Queen, even if the mob's was very similar. He was soliciting their vote; she was not. He actively provoked the mob; she did not. His wounds were real; hers, if any, were unknowable.

What is new in our present situation is that the elite, or an important part of it, has gone over, or has pretended to go over, to the mob's way of feeling. When Mr Blair called Diana 'the People's Princess,' he was performing a subtle and clever political manoeuvre, though perhaps he was unaware of its implications himself, just as a good footballer does not know the physics of curving a free kick.

Nothing could be clearer than that Mr Blair has himself no desire to live either among, or like, the majority of his countrymen. For this one cannot entirely blame him: for who would not rather be rich than have the average or median income, or dispose of more than the average or median assets? Who would not rather live luxuriously than in cramped, or in beautiful rather than ugly, surroundings? Who would not rather holiday in the Caribbean than in Clacton-on-Sea? There are, no doubt, nature's self-sacrificers, who are indifferent to their own comfort and welfare, but Mr Blair is not one of them, nor can he or anyone else be criticised for not being one of them. His ambition in respect of wealth and luxury is not dissimilar from that of millions of other people, inglorious though such ambition may be from an elevated philosophical point of view.

However, his means of lifting himself above the common herd has been to espouse, for political purposes, an especial concern for and empathy with the common herd, what he once called 'the many, not the few.' He has been careful to avoid any hint that he has cultural tastes that differ in any way from theirs. When he tells us that he is a supporter of Newcastle United football team, his real message is that 'I am not a snob or an intellectual, I am just like you, I like the same things as you, which is why I understand and feel for you.' It does not matter for his purposes whether or not he really is interested in Newcastle United, though his fantasies or lies about memories of having watched the famous player, Jackie Milburn, suggest that his protestations of deep interest are authentically bogus.

Certainly, no taint of high culture, as against high living, has ever attached to him. He has been careful to be photographed wearing jeans as well as suits, and holding a guitar, not a violin. Early in his premiership, he consorted with minor celebrities of popular culture as if fulfilling the dream of someone who had long (and longingly) read people magazines. Whether any of this represented his true interests, or was only part of a campaign of public relations, is unimportant; it was clearly of importance to him and his career.

Nor was he alone: the members of his first cabinet

admitted to no interests outside politics other than football. This in itself was a significant shift: many of the old Labour politicians, however misguided one might consider their economic and social policies to have been, were men of culture.

The death of the princess served Mr Blair's turn extremely well, and he seized the opportunity with skilful alacrity. She had precisely the combination of glamour and banality, with no threatening intelligence or refinement of taste, that was required by the new dispensation of populist elitism. Under cover of cultural similarity to the masses and democratic sentiment, the new elite would live a life as remote from that of the great majority of people as that of the aristocracy had ever been: indeed, more remote, in so far as the aristocracy had had to deal with the ordinary people on their estates. It was not a coincidence that Mr Blair was simultaneously the most populist and the most remote and inaccessible of modern Prime Ministers.

The sentimentality, both spontaneous and generated by the exaggerated attention of the media, that was necessary to turn the death of the princess into an event of such magnitude thus served a political purpose, one that was inherently dishonest in a way that parallels the dishonesty that lies behind much sentimentality itself.

A populist elitist such as Mr Blair cannot admit in public, and perhaps not even to himself, that he wishes above all to live the high life, as different from ordinary people as possible, among the rich and famous, preferably being rich and famous himself. This means that he has to give to his ambition a veneer of social purpose, in the process denying its very essence, its *fons et origo*. Overheated rhetoric, intellectual contortions and many forms of dishonesty are the inevitable result.

Mass sentimentality plays into the hands of demotic elitists, who are an elite only in their superior willingness to resort to the black arts of manipulation and bureaucratic in-fighting.

5

The Cult of the Victim

The *Guardian* newspaper issued a while ago a series of seven booklets inserted daily for a week in the newspaper, each devoted to one of the great poets of the twentieth century. The booklets contained an brief introduction and a few of the poets' best poems. One of the poets was Sylvia Plath, and in the introduction the novelist Margaret Drabble said:

> [Plath] embodied a seismic shift in consciousness which enabled us to feel and think as we do today, and of which she was a supremely vulnerable and willing casualty.

Supreme vulnerability and willingness to be a casualty, a victim, it is safe to assume, are here accounted virtues of a high order. Certainly, they are not invoked as a criticism.

Sylvia Plath was the daughter of a German-born father, Otto Plath, who was a man of considerable accomplishment, a university teacher of biology. Unfortunately, he died when his daughter was only ten years old. This, of course, was tragic, but it was (if I may so put it) a commonplace tragedy, the kind of thing that has been happening to people from time immemorial, and will continue happening until the human race is extinct.

Plath was a good, and some might even say a great, poet. But I doubt that her fame is now entirely due to her poetry. The domestic drama of her life, married as she was to a man who was an English poet inferior to herself, and that ended in her suicide by putting her head in the gas oven, has a deep appeal for those wishing to invest their own personal, domestic and relational tribulations with a significance beyond their immediate compass. She has therefore become the patron saint of self-dramatization.

One of the most famous of the poems in her most famous collection of poems, *Ariel*, which was first published in 1965, is entitled Daddy. In it, she apostrophises her dead father and, though from the 'objective' point of view she was much more fortunate than millions, perhaps tens of millions, of her countrymen, his early death notwithstanding, she blames him for her own suffering. In the poem, she describes her efforts to escape from his influence which, of course, is more by absence than by presence. Because of his

German background, and for no other reason, she identifies him with Nazism:

> If he was a Nazi, it is not surprising that his
>   daughter-victim was a Jew:
> I thought every German was you.

This is not the only time she assimilates herself to the Jews who suffered the Holocaust. In the poem Lady Lazarus, which refers to her own survival of her own suicide attempts, and which contains the famous lines:

> Dying
> Is an art, like everything else.
> I do it exceptionally well...

She writes that, after one such attempt:

> My face a featureless, fine
> Jew linen.

While it might be objected that poetic imagery is not intended to be taken literally — no one supposes, for example, that *Hamlet* could be literally compressed and imprisoned within a nutshell, and yet count himself king of infinite space — I think there is little doubt of the sincerity of the self-pity in Plath's poems.[34]

It is not a miracle of any kind that someone should survive a suicide attempt; on the contrary, the great majority of people who make such an attempt survive it.[35] As to the reference to human skin and lampshades, it eradicates the moral distinction between immolating oneself and being immolated.

Again, it might be objected that, since suffering is inherently subjective, no one is entitled to dismiss anyone's comparison of his own suffering with that of others. It is a commonplace of human observation that what is tolerable to one person is intolerable to another; people vary in their sensitivity and, as the poet Gerard Manley Hopkins put it of mental depression, 'No worse, there is none.' In other words, your situation is abominable if you think it is. There is in fact no way of distinguishing between the suffering of Sylvia Plath, brilliant scholar and citizen of a free country, and that of an involuntary resident of the Lodz ghetto.[36]

This might at first sight appear a deeply imaginative and compassionate doctrine, but the reality is quite otherwise: it is, or at any rate can be (as we shall see), a mask for the most complete indifference to the suffering of others. It means that all suffering must be taken at the sufferer's own estimate of it, which means that he is taken to suffer most who expresses himself most forcefully, or at any rate vehemently. It matters not what the source of the suffering is. If we are not allowed to judge a person's declamation of suffering by measuring it against his situation, for example by comparing it with the situation of another portion of humanity, then we leave no work for the imagination to do and we need make no empathetic leap: we rely purely on what is stated. We have no concept of suffering in silence; and, at the same time, we are forced to join in everyone's self-pity. It is hardly surprising if, in order to attract the attention of our sympathy, people feel obliged to claim untold suffering, even from the most banal and ordinary, indeed unavoidable, frustrations and disappointments that are consequent upon human existence. And just as people who fake illnesses begin to feel ill if they continue with their pretence long enough, for living as an invalid is not healthy for a healthy man, and in any case people do not like to consider themselves frauds, so people who claim loudly to suffer greatly from trivial causes eventually do suffer. The imagination brings reality into line with itself.

In order to attract the attention of the reader to her suffering, to her existential angst, Plath felt it right to allude to one of the worst and most deliberate inflictions of mass-suffering in the whole of human history, merely on the basis that her father, who died when she was young, was German. Her connection with the Holocaust was tenuous, to say the least; but her use of it for rhetorical purposes implied not only the scale of her suffering, but also its source, as being in some way of historical or political significance. This is ironical, because she was more apolitical than socially and politically engaged.[37]

In fact, the metaphorical use of the holocaust measures not the scale of her suffering, but of her self-pity,[38] which one might almost call heroic. Not very long before the publication of *Ariel*, at least in historical terms, self-pity was regarded as a vice, even a disgusting one, that precluded sympathy, though of course a permanent human temptation. Here, to take an example at random, is a passage from John Buchan's last book, *Sick Heart River*. The protagonist, Leithen, is dying of tuberculosis — as Buchan himself was when he wrote the book, dying only a few weeks after its completion. Leithen is reviewing his life, outwardly a successful one, but childless and without human warmth:

> He had made a niche for himself in the world, but it had been a chilly niche. With a start he awoke to the fact that he was very near the edge of self-pity, a thing forbidden.

Leithen did not allow himself the luxury of self-pity even within the confines of his own skull, for he knew that internal indulgence would lead before very long to external expression. As I used to tell medical students, they were not only not to call or refer to the old lady in the third bed on the left as Betty, but they were not to think of her as such. For them, she was Mrs Smith.

The appropriation of the suffering of others to boost the scale and significance of one's own suffering is now a commonplace. It is an international trend: emotional dishonesty knows no boundaries. For example, there was the famous case of Binjamin Wilkomirski, who published a book entitled *Fragments*, which purported to be shards of memory from very early in his childhood when he lived in ghettoes in Poland and was deported to the extermination camps, where miraculously he survived, later to be brought to Switzerland to be adopted by a gentile family, the head of which was a rich and eminent doctor.

The book was received ecstatically in many countries, and won several prizes, but before long a Swiss journalist, Daniel Ganzfried, discovered that Wilkomirski was really Bruno Grosjean, and had never been in an extermination camp. (Indeed, his story was very implausible from the internal evidence alone, but people wanted to believe it.) *Fragments* was a work of fiction, not a memoir.

In fact, Grosjean's story was not altogether a happy one. He was born in 1941, the illegitimate son of Yvonne Grosjean who worked in the Omega watch factory. Yvonne herself was the daughter of a father who died early and an alcoholic mother, and was fostered at the age of six. Early in her pregnancy with Bruno, by a man seven years her junior who refused to marry her (in fact he was a minor when he made her pregnant), she had a serious accident while riding a bicycle that left her unconscious for several weeks and both physically disabled and mentally slowed when she recovered. Although she tried to look after and provide for little Bruno, she could not, and he was fostered at the age of two. Two foster placements broke down, but then, at the age of four, he was adopted by the childless bourgeois doctor and his wife.

Wilkomirski, who grew up as Dosseker, the name of

his adoptive parents, became a musician. He later claimed that the Dossekers, now dead, had erased all traces of his Jewishness, cruelly forbidding any contact with the religion or culture of his birth. Of course, they were unable to rebut these allegations; the evidence seems to be that they were correct, if slightly distant, parents, who gave their child a privileged upbringing. During his childhood, Wilkomirski-Dosseker never left Switzerland.

Fragments contained memories, or rather supposed memories, of frightful events — which, of course, Wilkomirski could not have witnessed and must have imagined:

> They've put a man against the wall next to the front gate… He looks down at me and smiles. But suddenly his face clenches, he turns away, he lifts his head high and opens his mouth wide as if he's going to scream out… No sound comes out of his mouth, but a big stream of something black shoots out of his neck as the transport squashes him with a big crack against the house.

And so on.

One of the most extraordinary aspects of the whole affair was Wilkomirski's emotional meeting with a woman in California called Laura Grabowski, who claimed to have lived similar experiences to those of Wilkomirski, and who participated in a Holocaust Children's Survivors' Group. She, too, was eventually brought up in a gentile household, where she was not allowed to utter the words 'Poland' or 'Jewish.' By the time of their meeting, Wilkomirski was so famous that the meeting was filmed by the BBC. They played a duet together in front of an audience, many of whom were survivors of the Holocaust, he on the clarinet, she on the piano. He also claimed that their meeting was in fact a reunion; they had been together both in the Majdanek extermination camp and in the same orphanage in Poland immediately after the ending of the war.

They were interviewed together by the BBC. Grabowski was asked how Wilkomirski had changed since their time together in the Polish orphanage. 'He is my Binje' she replied, nestling her head on his neck, 'that's all I know. He has my heart and soul and I have his heart and soul.'

Unfortunately for those who were deeply moved by this supreme exhibition of kitsch, Grabowski turned out to be a serial fantasist and self-promoter. Like Wilkomirski, she had never been anywhere near Majdanek as a child; she was neither Jewish nor Polish (though her adoptive maternal grandparents were Polish, of the name Grabowski), but American.

She turned out to have been, in a previous life as it were, a woman called Lauren Stratford, formerly Laurel Rose Willson, who had written an 'autobiography' entitled *Satan's Underground: The Extraordinary Story of One Woman's Escape* in which she claimed to have been the victim of satanic ritual abuse.[39] Born illegitimate, she had been adopted by well-to-do parents (this part of her story, remarkably similar to Wilkomirski's, was true). At the age of six, according to her account, her mother allowed her to be raped by men for months on end, and then was used for the purposes of making pornographic films. She remained well into adulthood in the clutches of pornographers, whose leader, a man called Victor, demanded that she take part in the ritual sacrifice of babies. She refused and was kept in a cage with snakes; a dead and skinned baby would be thrown into her cage every week. She gave birth to three children while in captivity, one of them murdered for the purposes of making a film, and another bloodily killed in front of her as a human sacrifice.[40] Her book sold 140,000 copies.

Thereafter, she wrote a self-help book entitled *I Know You're Hurting: Living Through Emotional Pain*, and a further autobiography entitled *Stripped Naked: Gifts for Recovery*,[41] in which she claimed to have developed multiple personalities, fortunately re-integrated into one with the help of psychotherapy.

She then transformed herself into Laura Grabowski, a victim of Dr Mengele, and managed to extract funds from various charities, including the Swiss Fund for Needy Victims of the Holocaust, before latching on to Wilkomirski.

In her book, *I Know You're Hurting*, the woman who was to become Grabowski wrote a perfect charter for the self-pitying and self-dramatising:

We, who are the victims and survivors, had to remain silent too long. We finally braved the outside world and broke our silence in cautious whispers. Now, some of you are listening to us, and some of you are believing us. But there are many who do not listen, and there are many who do not believe. There are a few of you who do not even believe that we exist! This is a tragedy.

The pity of this is that there have been and indeed probably still are groups of people whose past and present suffering is unrecognised or unmentionable. The delayed public recognition of child abuse is a case in point,[42] or, to take an example from another sphere altogether, that of the Harkis and their descendants in France.[43]

When bogus claims to victim status become frequent and well-publicised, they serve to reduce sympathy for those who have really suffered, and to induce a state of cynicism. And such bogus claims do appear to be growing more frequent. There was the case, for example, of a Belgian woman who called herself Misha Defonseca and wrote a purported memoir of the Holocaust years. Claiming to be Jewish, she said that she had gone in search of her parents, deported to the east from Belgium in 1941 (deportations from Belgium started in 1942). Between the ages of seven and eleven, she said she had walked 3000 miles through occupied Europe as far as the Ukraine, escaped from the Warsaw ghetto, and was befriended by wolves. Despite the intrinsic implausibility of her story, her book was translated into eighteen languages, turned into an Italian opera, and was made the subject of a French film.

It took ten years to expose Misha Defonseca as a fraud. Her real name was Monique De Wael, the daughter of Catholic parents, and she lived in Brussels throughout the war. Her father was a member of the Belgian resistance, but was captured when Monique was four. Under torture by the Gestapo, it is thought, he informed on his colleagues; Monique grew up with other relatives. In 1988, she moved to the United States.

Her book itself reveals perfectly the dialectic between sentimentality and brutality. It was first published by a tiny press in America, and provided with a cover of quite exemplary kitsch. It shows the supposed Misha, apparently naked, with windswept flaxen hair, with a black silhouette of bayonet-bearing German soldiers, and a foreground of four wolf-cubs, one of them plaintively baying the moon, fluffy little creatures with the warmer, reddish coloration of foxes.

A single episode illustrates to perfection the intimate connection between sentimentality and brutality (bear in mind that the following story is purely imaginary). Misha had been befriended by a female wolf whom she names Rita, who then brought her mate, a male wolf whom she names Ita, to see her. Misha says of Rita:

She'd come to me upon hearing my howl of pain,

she'd stayed near me these many weeks, and now she'd brought her mate to introduce us to each other. My heart filled with love and gratitude. Until then 'Maman' was a name I could give to no one but my real mother, but just now this protective animal was the closest thing I had to a mother. From that time on I called her 'Maman Rita.'

Shortly afterwards, Maman Rita is shot and killed by a hunter, who then strings her up outside his shack. Little Misha — eight years old at the time — is not only grief-stricken but outraged. Screaming 'Murderer! Murderer!' to herself, she creeps up to the hunter's shack, which is surrounded with detritus.

… There, lying on the ground… was a length of heavy metal pipe. I picked it up with both hands and crept around to the front of the house. The man in the chair had his eyes closed now, his boots off and his feet resting on an overturned wooden bucket. Before he knew what was happening, I had raised the pipe high over my head and smashed it down with all my strength on his knees. His head jerked forward and he shrieked in pain. I raised the pipe again and he lunged at me, clutching at my arms, trying desperately to make me stop. But there was no way I could stop. I struck him, again and again.

After this edifying episode of imagined juvenile brutality — no doubt Freud would have called it wish-fulfilment — we return to the sentimental mode. Having left the hunter 'inert and groaning on the ground,' the eight year-old Misha:

> ... went around to the side of the house. Maman Rita hung there without dignity, eviscerated, like a chicken in the butcher's window. I lifted her from the hook and set her gently on the ground. With my knife, I cut the rope that bound her back legs, then I lifted her as high as I could over my shoulder and half carried, half dragged her back to the woods
>
> With tears streaming down my cheeks, I bore her proud body down the path she and I had walked just the day before. Coming to a small clearing filled with feathery ferns I gently laid her down. With both hands I dug the soft earth under a pine tree until I made a shallow hollow, like the one I slept in each night. Then I gently set my friend in her bed, kissed the soft muzzle that had so many times comforted me, and covered her with earth, pine needles and leaves. Not wanting to let her go, I scooped up dirt from the grave and rubbed it on my face and into my hair. Then, kneeling there by the mound, I doubled over in a contraction of grief and wailed.

Misha is not alone in her sentimentality. On the back

cover of the book, the Education Director of the North American Wolf Foundation is quoted as saying: 'Beautiful. Misha's loving description of the true nature of wolves will dispel many myths and touch the soul of all who read it.'

I don't know much about wolves, and am quite prepared to believe that they are splendid creatures in their way; but in my time as a doctor I've seen quite a few people beaten with metal pipes and the like; and, at the risk of sounding sentimental, they have my sympathy.[44]

When Monique De Wael was exposed as a fraud, she was not wholly repentant. Indeed, she claimed that her book had a kind of truth, not the correspondence to reality kind of truth, but something deeper, or at least more appealing to her fellow self-pitiers and self-dramatisers. Her books, she said, was a story, 'my story':

It is not the true reality but it is my reality.

Since all realities are equally real, and therefore equally 'valid,' to make use of a term increasingly resorted to by the ignorant when addressing themselves to the knowledgeable, she had subtly put herself beyond criticism.

She went on to say, with that mixture of candour and imprecision that is typical of those who want to talk about themselves without revealing anything:

There are times when I find it difficult to

differentiate between reality and my inner world.

A psychiatric excuse is here hinted at, and as we know it is wrong to criticise, stigmatise or express prejudice against the mentally ill; though it is doubtful whether Monique De Wael would wish actually to be considered psychotic. The psychotic, after all, find it impossible to distinguish between reality and their inner world, whereas she finds it only difficult. She wants sympathy, but not the men in white coats.

She went on to excuse what some have inaccurately called a hoax by reference to her life:

> My parents were arrested when I was four. I was taken in by my grandfather, Ernest De Wael, then by my uncle Maurice De Wael. They called me 'the traitor's daughter' because my father was suspected of talking under torture at St Gilles prison. Other than my grandfather, I hated those who took me in. They treated me badly.

In other words, she appeals to our sentimentality to excuse her for what she did, which is to have appropriated the occurrence and memory of mass murder for her own personal purposes, psychological and no doubt financial. Because she suffered and was badly treated as a child (let us give her the benefit of the doubt that must arise about anything she might now say about her own past), she begs our indulgence over a fraud committed more than half a century later. And, of course, there is the question of her 'reality:'

> I always felt different. It's true that, since forever, I
> felt Jewish and later in life could come to terms
> with myself by being welcomed by part of this
> community.[45]

Why and in what sense did she, and Dosseker-Wilkomirski, feel Jewish? It is highly unlikely that it had anything to do with the truth of Jewish religious doctrine.[46] They wanted to be Jewish because they thirsted for the condition of victimhood, and the genuine difficulties that they had faced in life were not of sufficient dimension to claim any great status in what one might call the community of victims. Their early path in life had not been easy, but they were born into a world in which, alas, millions of people had suffered worse, and far worse; and since they could not beat them, they joined them.

It must not be supposed, however, that the only group of victims to which self-pitiers or self-dramatisers wish to attach themselves is the survivors of the Holocaust. For example, Rigoberta Menchu, the Nobel prize-winning author, or co-author, of *I, Rigoberta Menchu*, considerably augmented her sufferings and altered the reasons for them, as a result coming to represent in the eyes of the world the indigenous population in Guatemala who suffered horribly during the civil war unleashed in that country by middle class intellectuals (including the son of the country's only other Nobel prize-winner). Of course, there are some who might say it does not really matter much whether Rigoberta Menchu herself suffered in exactly the way she described, so long as someone, or indeed many people, did; but it is surely not a matter of complete indifference if would-be leaders claim to have suffered what others have suffered, and in the process mis-attribute the source of those sufferings, in order to advance themselves.[47].

Not all claims to victim status are directly political. For example, in 2007 a woman who called herself Margaret B. Jones published a memoir entitled *Love and Consequences*. Hers was indeed a dramatic story. Allegedly half-white and half-Indian, at the age of six she was noticed by her teachers to be bleeding vaginally; they assumed that she had been the victim of a sexual assault in her home, and was therefore placed in the care of the local authorities, who fostered her out to a black woman called Big Mom in a rough part of Los Angeles. Her family story was one long tragedy: a brother Terrell was killed by a violent gang called the Crips, her sister NeeCee hanged herself. The narrator went to the bad and was dealing in drugs by the age of twelve to help out financially, in which capacity she witnessed a great deal of gang violence.[48]

The book gathered ecstatic reviews (it is in any case very difficult to write critically of accounts of severe suffering, for to do so is a little like kicking a man when he is down). The author allowed a profile of herself to be

173

published in the *New York Times*, complete with photograph, which unfortunately for her was recognised by her sister. Margaret B. Jones was really Margaret Seltzer, who, it turned out, had grown up in comfortable middle class circumstances, attending expensive and exclusive private schools and progressing through life without obvious external difficulties.

In explaining her daughter's repudiation of her actual comfortable middle class background for an imaginary one of sordid suffering, the author's mother said:

> I think she got caught up in the facts of the story she was trying to write. She's always been an activist and she tried to draw on the immediacy of the situation and became caught up in the persona of the narrator.

The woolliness and imprecision of the language suggest that the speaker is nervous and not very sure of her ground. The word activist is meant to convey to us the essential goodness of the young woman: she cares about the state of the world and wants to do good. (This, of course, does not recognise that activism is responsible also for a lot of the evil in the world as well as the good, so that activism is not in itself a good thing. The idea that activism is intrinsically good, and therefore excuses a lot, is itself a deeply sentimental one.)

The profile of the so-called Margaret B. Jones in the *New York Times* is rich mine for those interested in modern forms of sentimentality and the connection between such sentimentality and brutality. Entitled *Refugee from Gangland*, it carried a photograph of Ms Jones (sic) in the background, with her daughter and a black man in the foreground. The caption quotes her as saying that 'To me the family is a little broader than to the average person,' and goes on to inform us that she had taken in the man as a lodger to help him recover from a gunshot wound.

According to the writer of the profile:

She is one of the few people who in the same conversation can talk about the joys of putting up your own jam ('I'm going to give you a couple of jars!') and the painful business of getting tattooed a large, weeping pit bull across her back the day the state of Nevada set a close friend's execution date.

Here a sentimental metonym for domesticity, jam-making, is swiftly followed by a metonym for the brutality of the urban world of South Los Angeles, the pit bull, a breed of dog outlawed in many jurisdictions because of the vicious temperament for which it is esteemed in that world.[49] As if to underline the point, the dog — which is quite often in the news for having savaged and killed a baby — is weeping, not snarling or fixing its teeth into human flesh. The dialectical relationship between sentimentality and brutality could hardly be better expressed. Finally, the notion of tattooing oneself as a means of expressing one's feeling for another is both savage and sentimental, a sign of an empty heart's search for emotion.[50]

The relationship between sentimentality and brutality is further emphasised by the author of the profile, who says of *Love and Consequences*:

Unlike several other recent gang memoirs, all written by men, Ms. Jones' story is told from a nurturer's point of view. Along with grit and blood, every chapter describes tenderness and care between people.

Ms Jones, as she was then still calling herself, describes how happy she is to be living somewhere decent. 'Shoot, I'm happy,' she said to the writer from the *New York Times*. 'I'm making do. At least I'm not in three rooms any more.'

Her child, she said, was the result of her liaison with the first white man who dated her. When her baby was born, 'she was the first white baby she'd ever seen.' 'I said, she looks sickly, is there something wrong with her?'

She attributed her successful escape from the ghetto to the fact that she put the money she made from drug dealing (the only hope of economic advancement for people in the ghetto) towards her education rather than the purchase of a flashy car to impress others with. She went instead to Oregon University, there obtaining a degree in 'Ethnic Studies.'

She was not a complete class traitor, however. She confided to the writer from the *New York Times* that she 'still keeps up with gangland style, slang and people from her old life.' In other words, 'gangland style' has something, morally or aesthetically, to recommend it.

Sentimentality seeps through everything Margaret Seltzer did, said and wrote like treacle through sponge pudding. Her stunt is based upon the assumption that an upbringing in South Los Angeles is in some way more authentic, more 'real,' than one in comfortable suburban conditions; that it confers upon the person who has experienced it a special moral authority and right to be listened to with respect and even awe; that some people are so downtrodden or browbeaten by life that in criminality is their only hope of redemption; that somewhere in the hard crust of violence and brutality, there is a rich vein of kindness. Needless to say, 'ethnic studies' is the perfect course for a sentimentalist to study: the very existence of the subject requires a sentimental outlook on life.

When Margaret B. Jones turned out to be Margaret Seltzer, the publisher of her book withdrew all copies from the bookshops and offered to refund purchasers what they had paid for it (provided, of course, that they could furnish proof of purchase).[51] This was not the only time in recent years that a publisher has felt obliged to refund the cost of a memoir to its purchasers because of misdescription of its nature.

In 2000, a young American called James Frey had published what purported to be a factual account of his own addiction to alcohol and drugs, an addiction that had resulted in many criminal acts and a great deal of conflict with the law. He portrayed his own life as one of excess, vomit, and retribution.

The book was taken up by America's television queen of emotional incontinence, Oprah Winfrey, and became a best-seller. *A Million Little Pieces* sold at least 3,700,000 copies in the United States alone, more than any other book that year. It is reported that the staff of Oprah Winfrey's television programme were enjoined to read the book at home and would return the next day, their hearts bursting with what they had read and with tears in their eyes: the first rule of modern life being that one should not waste one's tears in private, but rather cry when others can see one.

Alas, it was soon discovered that the author had exaggerated grossly; and that, while hardly a pillar of respectable society, he was far from the debauched criminal he had made himself out to be, inveigled into the ways of wickedness by a condition of which he was the hapless victim, as are so many millions of others, namely a physiological addiction. Like others of his ilk, he had had a relatively privileged early life. His wrongdoing was petty, his travails minor; he was no romantic hero who had been plunged by the horror of his circumstances and experiences into the stormy depths; nor had he heroically clawed his way back to the dull but comfortable and temperate plains of normality.

As the late, and surprisingly lamented, President of Zaire, Marshal Mobutu Sese Seko[52] used to say, it takes two to be corrupt. In other words, books in which authors claimed the status of victim could be the path to social and financial success only in a social and cultural environment in which victimhood was seen as something heroic in itself. Whereas people once thirsted to read of the exceptional feats of explorers of Africa, or mappers of the untrodden wilderness, they now want to read of people who are known as, and call themselves, survivors of trauma. It seems hardly to matter that, in most cases, the experiences they 'survive' could not possibly have killed them and that, except in so far as they did not commit suicide, they could hardly have failed to survive; and that therefore their survival was scarcely more of an achievement than the drawing of breath.

Of course, the old heroes had often experienced terrible or horrifying things in the course of their adventures: but the exhibition of such experiences was not in itself the whole purpose of their narrations. Triumph over adversity was regarded as admirable, but the adversity to be triumphed over had to be exceptional rather than the common lot of mankind, or at least of very large numbers of people.

The romantic cult of sensibility gave moral authority to the suffering person. A person who did not suffer became a person of deficient character. He lacked both imagination and feeling. Indeed, virtue was thought to grow out of suffering: in 1950, Bertrand Russell thought it necessary to write an essay attacking the notion that the oppressed were possessed of superior virtue precisely because of their experience of oppression.[53]

History conspired to reinforce the romantic view. Technical progress notwithstanding, many of the worst episodes of barbarism in history occurred in the Twentieth Century.[54] Of these, those committed by the Nazis have been uppermost in everyone's mind. The German social philosopher, Theodore Adorno, famously remarked that after Auschwitz, there could be no more poetry.

What he meant by this, I suppose, is that the historical catastrophe was so great that it became the only proper subject of thought and feeling, at least for writers who claimed to be engaged intellectually and morally with the fate of mankind. In a world in which Auschwitz happened, and might very well happen again, it was trivial to concern oneself with such minor matters as the relations between men and woman in an unhappy marriage (a subject of a rich pre-Auschwitz literature), or prose style, or indeed anything else except genocide or the murder of millions.

There is an initial plausibility about this, or a seeming undeniability. To be more interested in the harmful effect of greenfly on roses than in the deliberate slaughter of millions appears frivolous and callous. To aver that one has no particular interest in the origins, causes, outcome and consequences of the Holocaust, but that one is very interested in the ceramic art of Andrea della Robbia, can give the impression of having a perverted scale of values, according to which the products of man, or at least some of the better products of man, are accorded more importance than man himself.

Yet the idea that there can be no poetry after Auschwitz (or any other event in human history) is utterly false, and is a powerful stimulus to insincerity and sentimentality. This is because it demands of people what is not possible for them; they have to pretend to feel what they cannot feel. However important a subject of study and reflection the Nazi atrocities may be, no one, not even a specialist, can devote every moment of his attention to them. You might as well say that there can be no good meals after Auschwitz as there can be no poetry after it: something that is patently absurd. Indeed, as a matter of historical fact the emphasis on the Holocaust as the defining event of European or world history was delayed until several decades after the ending of the war.

Moreover, a world in which everyone apportioned his attention and concern to subjects in precise proportion to their moral or historical significance would be an intolerable and deeply impoverished world. For example, there would be no veterinary surgeons to treat pet dogs (there would be no pet dogs, for that matter); there would be no experts on Byzantine history or on the archaeology of Angkor Wat. All the amenities of civilisation would cease; and a narrow moralistic monomania would become the mark of the good man.[55] It need hardly be pointed out that this would be an open invitation to the worst kind of hypocrisy.

Notwithstanding the impossibility, insincerity and absurdity of the idea that the occurrence of Auschwitz changed everything, it was nevertheless so genuinely appalling an occurrence that it conferred a special status on its victims, as having a moral authority to speak of the ultimate questions of existence possessed by no one else. Some of its victims did indeed possess special moral authority: Primo Levi springs here to mind. But that authority could not have derived from their sufferings alone; it was their response to their sufferings, and those of innumerable others, that gave them their authority.

Nevertheless, the habit of listening with uncritical awe to those who have suffered greatly, purely on account of their sufferings, probably started after the Second World War, and became a culturally-ingrained habit. It is indeed psychologically difficult to contradict someone known to have suffered greatly: I have myself listened to people who have been horribly tortured or abused and who have said things that were plainly mistaken, because logically inconsistent with other things that they have said, without daring to point out the contradictions. In part this was because I desired to cause them no further suffering. They might easily have concluded, had I mentioned the contradictions, that I did not believe the essence of their story; and it takes little effort of the imagination to understand how agonising it must be to have had the severest suffering inflicted upon one and yet not to be believed.[56] But I also kept my counsel because I felt acutely that, never having suffered anything comparable myself, I was not in a moral position to contradict them, however logical or well-founded my objections. Their opinions counted for more than mine precisely because of what they had experienced. The right to an uncontradicted opinion was earned by suffering.

I knew this to be an irrational idea, but one that has become widely accepted. Only the person who has experienced suffering has the right to speak of it; and he has special authority conferred by that suffering. Thus if I told a drug addict withdrawing from opiates that such withdrawal was not a serious medical condition, he was more likely than not to reply that, never having experienced it myself, I had no standing to speak of its seriousness. I pointed out that there were many conditions that, as a doctor, I knew to be serious though I had never experienced them myself, and likewise with trivial ones; that I was in regular contact with people who suffered incomparably worse; and that experimental evidence suggested that a very considerable proportion of the suffering induced by withdrawal, in so far as it was not exaggerated to deceive doctors and others, was caused psychologically by anticipation and expectation rather than the mere fact of pharmacological abstinence. His own declamation of suffering trumped all other evidence both as to its source and its degree.

The elevation of the status of the suffering victim occurred in the west not when real and terrible mass victimisation was of very recent memory, but when Western Europe and America seemed to have recovered from the worst excesses of such victimisation, and indeed were prospering. Sylvia Plath had not been a victim of anything, or at least of anything political, when she used imagery from the Holocaust to describe her own case; within a few years of the publication of her poems, the well-heeled and fashionably dressed students of Paris were chanting such slogans as 'We're all German Jews.' The students drew cartoons of General De Gaulle with his physiognomy as a mask behind which was the real face of Hitler, with the implication that the Fifth Republic was some kind of covert Nazi dictatorship of which the students were the oppressed victims.[57] Far from being victims, they were the very elite of the country, destined before very long to reach positions of social, economic and political power. But they were pioneers in what became a cultural trend: the desire and ability of the privileged to see themselves as victims, and therefore endowed with incontrovertible moral authority. And in a democratic age, the less privileged will soon do what the privileged do. Before long, a sense of victimhood became almost universal: everyone was a victim of something, gross or subtle as the case might be. It even became quite common to argue that subtle victimisation was worse than gross, because it was less visible and therefore more difficult to resist.

This was fostered by the idea that a victim is a person who believes that he is a victim. No objective evidence that he is a victim is required. For example, one of the recommendations of the official inquiry into the murder of Stephen Lawrence.[58] was that the definition of a racist incident should be:

... any incident which is perceived to be racist by the victim or any other person.[59]

There is no requirement that the perception should have any objective and publicly observable correlates; on this definition, the evidence of a schizophrenic who hears voices in the air establishes the racist nature of an incident as firmly as a hundred witnesses who have recorded faithfully what was said and done. As Mrs Lawrence, the mother of the murdered young man, pointed out in her evidence to the inquiry when asked whether the police had dealt with her in a racist way:

Racism is something you can't always just put your finger on. Racism is done in a way that is so subtle. It is how they talk to you... It is just the whole attitude... It was patronising the way in which they dealt with me and that came across as being racist.

It is, of course, entirely understandable from the psychological point of view that Mrs Lawrence should have been feeling highly sensitive at the time: what mother who had lost a son in such a way, particularly when the culprits had not been found and convicted, and were now never likely to be found and convicted, would not have been highly sensitive?

Since elsewhere in the report it is recommended that a person should be defined as a member of an ethnic minority if he considers himself such, and since crimes that are considered racially-motivated are also deemed to be aggravated, thereby attracting a heavier sentence, it is clear that the report recommends that, potentially at least, a purely subjective feeling on the part of a victim could and should have a determining effect upon the punishment of the culprit. Furthermore, the report recommends that in such cases the ancient rule against double jeopardy — that a man should not be tried for the same crime twice — should be abrogated. When the victim, or the victim's close relatives, feel strongly enough about it (provided they are members of an appropriate and accredited racial victim group), there should be no such thing as a final acquittal.

It is unfair that the words of Mrs Lawrence — those of an understandably grieving and angry woman — should have been published, because their publication, especially when used entirely sentimentally as evidence in favour of practical recommendations that, if implemented, would so fundamentally undermine the rule of law, makes it necessary that they and their underlying assumptions should be carefully analysed.

When Mrs Lawrence says that the way in which she was treated was patronising she might have been right; that, certainly, is how she felt. But the fact that she felt as if she were being patronised is not evidence in itself that she was in fact patronised. Some people are hypersensitive to slights, and see them where none was intended (though, equally, some do not see them when they are).

Furthermore, patronising attitudes are bound to increase in a cultural atmosphere in which a slight is deemed to be a racial one if someone merely takes it into his head to deem it so, an atmosphere that the report was dedicated to fostering.

As if this were not enough, there can be patronising attitudes in the absence of racial motivation. Indeed, it was a common complaint among my patients who had been victims of a crime that the police were either indifferent or patronising towards them. If they condescended to investigate a burglary, for example, they often implied that the victim had been careless in securing his possessions: that he ought to have had more locks on his doors, in the absence of which he must expect to be burgled. It was quite unreasonable of him to expect the criminal justice system to protect him and his property; it has far more important things to do.

It is not a criticism of Mrs Lawrence that she failed to see the complexities of the question, or to understand how dwelling upon it might actually make the situation worse in the future, in so far as it makes ordinary and unselfconscious human relations impossible. She, after all, was merely a witness, and not an author of the report. Furthermore, she was in a situation with which anyone could sympathise, that of a mother whose son's murder had been poorly investigated. But there is no such excuse for the stupid and vicious sentimentality of the authors of the report who say:

The fact that [Mr and Mrs Lawrence] were in their eyes and to their perception patronised and inappropriately treated exhibits plain but unintentional failure to treat them appropriately and professionally within their own culture and as a black grieving family.

The irony is completely unnoticed that this passage suggests that black and white families mourn murdered sons in some very different way, and by doing so also suggests that black and white have fundamentally different psychologies — precisely what the most ardent racist would allege,[60] for in what response could, say, black and white mothers be more similar than in that to the unexpected murder of a beloved son?

No person of goodwill can doubt that racism existed and still exists, especially among individuals. I remember a patient of mine, who came from Jamaica to Britain in the 1950s, who found a job in the staff canteen of a hospital. She told me (and I believed her, though not because she was black, but because she struck me as a truthful person), that some of the staff of the hospital, never having seen a black person close-up before and imbued with all kind of ideas about blacks, refused to eat any of the food in the preparation of which she had had a hand. Her response had been to make her cooking so good that she would overcome this prejudice, and before long the staff that refused to eat her food would eat no other.

Of course, there were instances of racism both in the

distant and recent past that were worse and less easily overcome than this; but none of those instances justified or could ever justify treating with reverence the opinions of individuals within groups that were once, or still are, the object of unfair discrimination, as if they were sacrosanct and without further need of justification. Exactly how dangerous this sentimental way of thinking is, at least potentially, and just how destructive of rationality and the rule of law, is revealed by the report on the murder of Stephen Lawrence. It will be remembered that the report suggested that a racist incident should be defined as one which any witness to it considered to be racist; it also suggested that there should be in place 'strategies for the prevention, recording, investigation and prosecution of racist incidents,' and that these strategies should be implemented throughout the public administration. Since earlier in the report it was acknowledged that racist incidents did not necessarily involve breaking any law, what is here proposed is a reign of arbitrary punishment of people for alleged acts or omissions, defence against which is logically impossible. Accusation and guilt have become entirely synonymous.

Not much effort of the imagination is required to understand the consequences of such proposals if implemented, which are thoroughly totalitarian in inspiration.[61] The idea that victims, real or imagined, should be given infinite power to determine the functioning of the public service would, of course, soon lead to demands for extension of that power to all parts of society. There is a very considerable element of sadism in all this (it would certainly end in violence), and once again the connection between sentimentality and brutality is exposed.

The habit of taking alleged victimisation at its own estimate is now a common one. For example, in one hospital of which I had knowledge before my retirement, staff who complained of having been bullied could take comfort from the hospital personnel department's official definition of bullying: a person was being bullied if he thought that he was being bullied. Once again, there was no requirement that, to establish the justifiability of a complaint, there should be objective evidence of the behaviour complained of: a mere look, a tone of voice, a kind gesture, even nothing at all, indeed a total absence of any contact whatsoever, could be interpreted as bullying.

The correct idea that the powerless in any organisation need some protection against the powerful has here been sentimentally transformed into the idea that the less powerful are always accurate and truthful when it comes to their account of their relations with the more powerful. The sentimentalised idea is related to the supposition that, in any antagonism between 'ordinary' people and authority, the former must have right on their side.[62] It is often true, of course, that authority is to blame, and not 'ordinary' people, but it is not invariably true. Only if you believe in the sub-Rouseauean idea that it is high position in a hierarchy alone that introduces evil or narrowly self-interested intentions into human conduct it is possible to maintain the absolute moral distinction between ordinary people and authority.

Moreover, within the hospital to which I refer, it was perfectly clear that the supposed protection of the powerless was actually a means not of preventing or correcting abuse of power, but of transferring power from traditional authorities to new ones. The complaints of bullying had, after all, to be adjudicated; and it was the hospital managers, who had once been subordinate to senior doctors and nurses, who were the traditional authorities, who adjudicated. Their definition of bullying (and other crimes of the heart and tongue, such as racism and sexism) being so complainant-friendly, complaints became more common and called forth an immense apparatus of investigation and supposed reconciliation. Highly educated and trained men and women — it is not unusual for a doctor to have spent more than a third of a century in education and training before he reaches his final position of authority — found themselves spending a great deal of their time trying to rebut charges of a Kafka-esque nature[63] brought by someone who had taken offence at the slightest of slights, or none at all. In these circumstances, the very triviality of the allegations was advantageous to the administration in the transfer of power: for if a giant investigative and quasi-judicial apparatus swung into operation on so trivial an occasion, it meant that every move, indeed every word, was under potential surveillance. The power of the former authorities was broken with surprising swiftness and completeness, without there having been any formal revolution, and despite the fact that the former authorities had all the resources of tradition, intelligence and education on their side. But they never dared accuse their accusers of exaggeration, hysteria, lying and so forth: for to have done so would be not to have taken a self-declared victim at his or her word,[64] a sign of the urgent need for re-education.

The self-declared victim also seems to be at an advantage in civil actions in courts. There are, of course, powerful reasons why a litigant should become more and more embittered as a case progresses, or fails to progress, and why he should come to exaggerate the wrong allegedly done to him. It takes years for a case finally to come to court; as often as not, he has spent the intervening interval rehearsing his story of woe, reliving the alleged cause of his suffering, and rebutting contrary evidence entered by the defendant, to the exclusion of everything else in his life. But even when allowances are made for this process, the fact remains that many claims are so grossly disproportionate to any possible harm done that they can only be described as fraudulent. Yet in cases in which I have been involved, the judge has seemed reluctant to draw any inference about the plaintiff who claims many, many times the loss than could reasonably and rationally have been claimed. One cannot resist the impression that the doctrine that a person who has been harmed in some way is a victim, and therefore cannot commit any wrong, has been turned into a money-spinner by lawyers.

Likewise, the legal doctrine that psychological damage is not conceptually and juridically different from physical damage is both sentimental about the nature of mankind, and highly advantageous to the legal profession. If a professional footballer is involved in an accident as a result of which one of his legs must be amputated, the harm done to his career is fairly obvious and indisputable. His future earnings could be calculated with a fair degree of likelihood. But if a man is involved in a trivial accident as a result of which he claims that he is too frightened to leave his house, it is clear that the hope of gain might easily affect his reaction to the accident.[65]

The extent to which the law is complicit in the manufacture of victims is clear from the following. A man, through no fault of his own, was briefly exposed to a harmful chemical. He claimed compensation; and by the time his case came to court not only had his symptoms worsened very considerably, but he claimed that the brilliant career that he was on the verge of starting when he was exposed to the chemical, of which there was absolutely no sign before, had been ruined once and for all. As a consequence, the sum that he claimed in compensation was huge, vastly in excess of any sum of money he might otherwise ever have accumulated.

In cross-examination it emerged that he developed his symptoms not after exposure to the chemical, but only after he had looked up the effects of that chemical on the internet. Naively, I supposed that that would be the end of the case; that it would be peremptorily dismissed as being little more than what protection rackets used to call a shake-down. But I was mistaken, and had made no allowance for the dishonesty of the law.

On the contrary, the law (as it then stood) held that the injuries were still a consequence of the original exposure to the chemical, for had he not been exposed to the chemical he would not have looked up the supposed effects on the internet. It hardly needs to be pointed out that this legal doctrine amounts to an open invitation to fraud; or perhaps it would be more accurate to say that it legalises fraud.

In effect the doctrine maintains that, once a person has become a victim, he is no longer responsible, psychologically, morally or legally, for his subsequent actions in so far as they have some causative connection with whatever it was that made him a victim in the first place.

This view of victimhood — that it removes from the victim the burden of responsibility, moral and sometimes legal — has become very widespread: so widespread, indeed, that the author of an intelligent and sensitive book about the legal consequences of Battered Wife Syndrome,[66] felt compelled to state: 'Surprisingly, trauma and reason can coexist.'

That trauma and reason can coexist could come as a surprise only to people who were firmly convinced of the opposite: that victimisation by its very nature deprives a person of all moral responsibility for anything, and that afterwards he becomes an automaton.

At the same time, and not quite logically, a person who has been victimised and yet behaves well, or at least refrains from behaving badly, is transformed into some kind of hero, like the mother who is starving but nevertheless declines to take food out of the mouths of her children: for he has resisted the temptation that the excuse of victimisation offers him for behaving in a thoroughly impulsive and egotistical way.[67]

From the fact, or supposed fact, that people who had been traumatised in some way tended as a consequence to behave afterwards in certain self-destructive or maladaptive ways, it was concluded that self-destruction or maladaption was itself evidence of traumatisation: else why would anyone behave like that? The logic was bad, of course: it certainly does not follow from the fact that some *a*s are *b*s that all *b*s are *a*s; but logic has not always played the part that it might have played in human affairs.

Bruno Bettelheim was instrumental, or at least an instrument, in establishing the connection between trauma, victimisation and bad behaviour. Before reaching the United States, he had spent just over ten months in Nazi concentration camps, when they were not yet holding posts for extermination camps. In *The Informed Heart*, his account of his time in the camps, he wrote:

The author saw his fellow prisoners acting in most peculiar ways, although he had every reason to assume that they, too, had been normal persons before being imprisoned: Now they suddenly appeared to be *pathological* liars, to be unable to restrain their emotional outbursts, be they of anger or despair, to be unable to make objective evaluations ...

Emotional outbursts eventually entered popular culture as *mood swings*, that is to say sudden rages or tantrums that are designed to blackmail or intimidate others. They are conceived to be rather like epileptic fits, and indicate deep psychological disturbance resulting from trauma and victimisation.[68]

The desire, or thirst, to be a victim has become so great that people now frequently claim to be victims of their own bad behaviour. Since every event is caused by something, it follows that all behaviour that leads to unfortunate or undesired consequences must be caused; and since a choice is also an event, it too must be caused. But since no one knows the origin of his own choices, everyone is a victim of circumstances that are beyond his control. It goes without saying that such thinking applies only to what needs to be explained away rather than merely explained.

The addict thus becomes a victim, and the worse the effects of his addiction, for himself and others, the more of a victim he is. No one, for example, is interested in the addiction of William Wilberforce to laudanum: he simply took a certain quantity of it every day and got on with his life, in many respects an exemplary one. James Frey, by contrast, was supposedly led by his addiction to the uttermost depths of degradation, and thereby became a hero, the very depth of the degradation being a proof of the depth of his victimhood. The more he covered himself with vomit, the worse the charges laid against him, the more worthy of pity he became.[69]

Suffering has become the mark of victimhood, however it originates. No distinction is drawn between that which is self-inflicted and that which is entirely fortuitous (let alone between all the subtle intervening gradations). To draw the distinction would be *judgmental*, which is judged to be the worst thing one could be, and so no judgment of this nature is made.

Now of course it is as easy to attribute blame to a truly helpless victim as it is to conceive of a moral agent as a complete victim. There are undoubtedly cases of victimisation — by natural forces beyond anyone's control, by oppressors — so great that the victim's choices are severely limited. I have known men so oppressive to their sexual consorts that they locked them up in a cupboard by day, never allowed them out on their own, and were unmercifully violent towards them. I have known fathers imprison, dominate, terrorise and abuse their daughters since birth, for decades on end. When finally the victim of a man who behaves in this fashion kills him from desperation, no person of normal compassion would put them in the same category as someone who, say, kills for life insurance money.

But most cases of victimisation are less clear-cut than

the ones suggested above, and most people make a larger contribution to their own unhappiness than they do in cases of pure and unadulterated victimhood. For example, women victims of abusive men are seldom victims and nothing more. As is well known, they are often highly ambivalent about their abuser; at the outset of their relationship, which they often started with insouciance, they refused to take heed of signs, or even in some cases certain knowledge, that he was a violent and abusive man;[70] they continue to accept his apologies and promises of change well after it is perfectly obvious that he has no intention of changing; they refuse offers of assistance to escape from him.

The suggestion that victims of vicious behaviour are sometimes complicit in it strikes many people as callous, when actually it is sentimental or demeaning, or both, not to acknowledge it. It turns adults into dolls, into mere simulacra of human beings, without thoughts or actions of their own; it suggests that they can do nothing to help themselves and it gives unlimited powers to those who claim, more often than not falsely, to be their protectors and saviours. And, oddly enough, the refusal to see the part that people play in their own downfall leads, in practice, to complete callousness and indifference to their suffering.

First, the notion that all who suffer are victims has the corollary — false in logic but psychologically very powerful — that those who are not victims do not suffer. Since victimhood is a status ascribed by membership of a social group that has had its victimisation certified, those who are not members of such a group are by definition not victims, do not suffer and are therefore not worthy of sympathy.

The idea that those who certifiably suffer are victims has a further undesirable corollary, namely that assistance should be rendered according to need and not according to desert. Again, at first sight this seems compassionate, for it avoids the need to distinguish between the deserving and the undeserving, a distinction that can easily be made in a harsh and censorious fashion or spirit, and moreover can be mistaken even when made with genuine compassion and goodwill.

The effort to avoid censoriousness is now so great that people who fake illnesses, or habitually tell preposterous lies, are diagnosed as ill, for almost any undesirable behaviour that falls into a recognisable pattern is given a label — as if, were it not for the unfortunate irruption of illness into people's lives, everyone would be a fine, upstanding citizen.

But the avoidance of moral judgment is in any case the mask of indifference and callousness. It is a psychological impossibility to be compassionate equally with all the people in the world who suffer, and the demand that we do so is in effect the demand that we do so with none. When I had cause in my hospital work to request the special and urgent attention of a social worker to the problems of a particular patient, my plea that the case was an especially deserving one was met with stony indifference. For if one case was especially deserving, that meant that other cases were, relatively-speaking, undeserving. And that, of course, undermined the doctrine that the origin of suffering is unimportant, since all is ultimately the consequence of victimisation. So I was told in no uncertain terms that my especially deserving case, so called, would have to wait his or her turn, and had no claims to special or privileged treatment.

The removal of desert as *a* criterion (but, as we shall see, not *the* criterion) for the allocation of assistance helps to deprive human life of any meaning, and to promote the most unbridled egotism: for if reward is disconnected from desert, consequences have no moral content, and ends may be pursued without regard to the interest of others.

The habit of making no judgment about desert leads to laziness and indifference. It is clearly not the case that people who are the authors of their own misfortune, either wholly or in part, are unworthy of assistance. No doctor, for example, would refuse to treat a man with *delirium tremens*, a condition with a significant death rate, because it was the consequence of his having chosen, over a long period, to drink too much (and experimental evidence suggests that drinking is always a choice, and never merely an automatic and ineluctable consequence of a state of addiction).

Quite often in the hospital in which I worked I had women patients who had been badly abused by their sexual consorts and who feared for their lives if they returned home, having been threatened by them with death. Their fears were far from unreasonable; their consorts were drunk, jealous and violent, the kind of men who, in quite disproportionate numbers, do kill women.

More often than not, the women who found themselves in this situation had been very foolish. They had met their tormentor in the pub and in some cases had agreed to live with him within a few minutes or hours of meeting him, knowing little of him but being able to guess by his appearance,[71] that he might be violently inclined; they had failed to leave him when his true character declared itself a first, second third or fourth time; they had called the police on innumerable occasions but withdrawn their allegations at the last moment, just as the case came to court.

But while it was important to draw their attention to their own foolishness which they often disguised from themselves (for how, except by acknowledging it, could they learn from experience?), it was also important to help them. Having decided, however belatedly, to leave their tormentors, who in some cases were lurking somewhere in the hospital for them, they needed somewhere to go, some shelter where their tormentors could not find them; but when I called the social workers for their assistance, they would say only that the woman concerned had to apply to the social services office nearest her residence, the normal procedure when someone requested public assistance in moving residence. In vain did I argue that the normal procedure was not appropriate in this case, that the woman was in terror of her life, for a good reason, and that the man who had threatened to kill her might easily find her if she returned to the area in which she lived. No, the procedure was the procedure, to go against which would be as sacrilegious as the setting up a golden calf had once been. It was therefore out of the question that the woman should receive special treatment just because she was under threat of death. What was good enough for one victim was good enough for another.

The psychological fact is that it is impossible to feel anything very much for millions of people, other than in a cold and abstract way. One death is a tragedy, said Stalin, a million deaths is a statistic, and he was right. That is why we still resort to individual memoirs to try to understand historical catastrophes. And where victimhood becomes the general condition of mankind, genuine compassion becomes impossible: it is like trying to spread half an ounce of butter over a million loaves of bread.

The reason why victimhood should have become so ardently sought and ascribed a status is traceable to the Romantic revolution of the second half of the Eighteenth Century. (Since history is a seamless robe, one may, of course, legitimately ask why that revolution took place.) At any rate, there was change in man's conception of himself, first among intellectuals, and then in the population as a whole, and change with whose effects we still live.

The Christian view, that man was born imperfect but could and should strive in person towards perfection, was first challenged and then replaced by the Romantic view that mankind was born naturally good but was corrupted into badness by living in a bad society. Thus the exhibition of vice became evidence of having been treated badly. What had been deemed moral defect became victimhood whether conscious or not; and since mankind was born happy as well as good, unhappiness and suffering were likewise evidence of bad treatment and victimhood. To restore men to their original and natural state of goodness and happiness, therefore, required social engineering on a huge scale. It is not surprising that the Romantic revolution should have ushered in the era of massacre for ideological reasons.

The Christian view is much less sentimental than the secularist.[72] The secularist sees victims everywhere, hordes of suffering people who need rescue from injustice.[73] In these circumstances, it has become advantageous to claim victimhood for oneself — psychologically and sometimes financially — because to be a victim is to be a beneficiary of injustice. This is why so many highly privileged people, who by the standards of all previously existing populations, lead lives of outstanding comfort, freedom and possibilities, claim the status of victim.

By contrast, the Christian view acknowledges that folly and wickedness are inescapably part of the human condition.[74] They vary in degree between individuals, but they inhere in all of us. That is why it is possible for someone who believes in Original Sin, the most useful of all myths, to be clear-sighted and compassionate at the same time, but very difficult for someone who believes in mankind's natural goodness, who forgives all because he claims to understand all, and then becomes indifferent and unfeeling.

An exemplar of clear-sightedness is Doctor Johnson. Far from a sentimentalist, he believed firmly in punishment, up to and including the death penalty, but yet he was able to write, with obviously deep and sincere feeling:

> The humanity of that man can deserve no panegyric, who is capable of reproaching a criminal in the hands of the executioner.

For the sentimentalist, of course, there is no such thing as a criminal, only an environment that has let him down.

6

Make Poverty History!

Make poverty history! Here the word 'history' is employed in the way in which a gangsterish person might employ it to someone of whose presence he wished to disembarrass himself. 'You're history!'[75]

And how is poverty to be eliminated from the repertoire of possible human conditions? Let us leave aside for one moment the definition of poverty, quite an important question in the context. The answer is obvious: aging pop stars are to give a series of concerts to youth with disposable incomes, and at the same time appeal to governments to tax the general population and donate the resultant money to the poorest countries, usually the governments of the poorest countries. This is despite the fact that most aging pop stars employ armies of accountants and tax lawyers to protect their huge incomes from the depredations of the tax authorities. We should remember that there are few pleasures greater than promoting your moral enthusiasms at other people's expense.

But what, exactly, is the poverty that is to be made history? Is it absolute poverty or relative poverty? Is it the kind of poverty in which women have to walk miles to the nearest source of water and do not have enough to feed their children, or is it the kind of poverty that exists so long as incomes are not equal, that is to say among people whose income is less than sixty per cent of that of the median income, a definition that is often used and means that, in a society of billionaires, a multi-millionaire could be considered poor? The answer is that it is sometimes the one, sometimes the other, depending upon the context.

If it is the latter, of course, poverty will never be history until there is equality, more or less. On this view, a society in which everyone has an income of $200 per year is less poor than one in which ninety per cent of the population has an income of $1,000,000 per year, but ten per cent have an income of only $300,000.

Even the measurement of absolute poverty has its difficulties: one measure often used by the World Bank, for example, is a notional income of less than $1.25 per day. But this cannot really mean anything, since an income of $1.25 per day in Stockholm or Moscow, or indeed in much of the world, would be quite insufficient to sustain life even for a single month, at least if no additional source of goods or income were available. And yet millions of people, indeed hundreds of millions of people (also according to the Bank), do survive for many years on such an income, or less. The definition doesn't make sense.

Still, it isn't all that difficult to recognise chronic absolute poverty when you see it, and it is also obvious that it is not a condition that is either desired or desirable. The disadvantages of absolute poverty are so obvious that they hardly need enumerating: a shortened life span, increased experience of physical illness, pain and disability without access to treatment or relief, unremitting and monotonous toil merely to survive even at a low level, insecurity and anxiety about the future, and so forth.

There seems little doubt that the proportion of mankind living in this kind of poverty has decreased dramatically in the past quarter century, the World Bank suggesting indeed that it has halved. The decrease has been most marked in India and China. Africa is an exception.

Africa, therefore, is the current focus of sentimentality about poverty. It has long been so: Dickens satirised it in *Bleak House*, Mrs Jellyby being so concerned for the education of the natives of the Borioboola-Gha, on the left bank of the Niger, that she entirely neglects her own children.

This precisely captures the stance of Gordon Brown, our previous Prime Minister. A man not normally given to excesses of self-promotion, several times he took care to have himself photographed on trips to Africa with local children. He declared it his goal to ensure that every child on the continent should have at least a primary education, without, apparently, understanding the irony of this. He was the leader of a country with a thoroughly disgraceful record with regard to the welfare of children.

Though not self-promoting in the obvious and vulgar way of his predecessor, he is nevertheless a politician, and one who must subject himself from time to time to elections.[76] He must therefore have understood that his posturing in Africa would appeal to a large constituency of voters, that a significant proportion of the population had become Jellybied. By such posturing, he would get a reputation among them of being a good man, one who *cared*, for in the modern world a good man is a man who has the right opinions and utters impeccable sentiments, his actual conduct being considerably less important. And who can possibly be against an improvement in the conditions of life for African children?[77]

The great development economist Peter Bauer pointed out a long time ago the dangers of using terms, such as 'aid,' that precluded debate about their presuppositions because the connotations of the terms were so positive that no one, except someone deeply vicious, could demur or dissent.

Let us just examine for a moment the presuppositions of Mr Brown's desire to bring education to African children. Some or all of them may be right, but equally some or all of them they might be wrong.

On his view, the low level of education in Africa inhibits economic growth. Africa is poor because the people are ignorant and illiterate. Remove the ignorance and teach them to read, a la Mrs Jellyby, and all will be well, or at least much better.

But is this so? Is there any correlation in Africa between levels of education and rates of economic growth? And even if there were such a correlation, could we be sure that it was education that caused growth rather than that growth caused education, or indeed that there was no causative relation at all.

I lived some years of my life in Tanzania, during the rule of its first president, much admired in certain quarters, Julius Nyerere. By comparison with many first-generation African dictators, there is no doubt that Nyerere had some important virtues. He was not a tribalist, favouring his own ethnic group over all others and thus creating or sharpening already existent ethnic antipathies. No doubt it helped that there were no numerically or economically dominant ethnic groups in the country (but this did not prevent some dictators, for example Samuel Doe of Liberia, from promoting members of his own minority ethnic group into positions of power, thus promoting tensions that ended in violence).[78] Though he had no objection to imprisoning large numbers of his opponents until he had no opponents, he was not obviously bizarre or bloodthirsty as many of his colleagues were. And, in the context, these were not small virtues.

Unhappily, however, Nyerere was seized by a view of the world not altogether dissimilar from Mr Brown's.[79] He, too, was a devotee of education. The achievements of his government in this respect were impressive: the level of literacy in his country swiftly improved under his rule, and probably reached the level of those of Britain. While Britain's levels of literacy were unimpressive for a developed country, Tanzania's were impressive for an African one.

Alas, this improvement in the levels of education contributed nothing to economic development. Tanzania under Nyerere grew successively poorer, despite many natural advantages and levels of international aid that, *per capita*, were the highest in Africa. Nyerere destroyed commercial farming by expropriation in the name of fairness, though there was actually no land hunger among the peasantry that could have provided even a superficial justification for this policy, he drove out most of the Indian traders by making conditions very difficult or impossible for them, and he moved seven tenths of the peasantry by force into semi-collectivised villages, a criminal idiocy that drew the hosannas of a certain kind of Third-Worldist. Having destroyed the system of private merchants on the (sentimental) grounds that they were exploitative of the peasants, because they paid less for the peasants' produce than they sold it on for (what else were they supposed to do?), Nyerere destroyed all incentive for the peasants to produce anything other than for their own subsistence. He set up state purchasing boards run and staffed by vast bureaucracies to buy crops from the peasantry at prices decreed by the government in a debased currency that would purchase nothing — 'Pictures of Nyerere' was what the peasants called the money. The result was that, though nine-tenths of the population lived on the land, the country was never self-sufficient even in food, let alone in anything else. Into the breach stepped the Mr Browns of the world. They paid for all this woeful economic incompetence.[80]

The high level of literacy did not improve the economic situation for two reasons, the first economic and the second cultural. The economic cost of raising literacy was considerable, and used up scarce resources; this would have been a good thing, from the economic point of view, only if it were in fact the case that a high level of education automatically results in economic development. Otherwise, such investment in education is economically harmful, because wasteful.

A high level of education was economically harmful for cultural reasons also. One of the legacies of colonialism, in Tanzania as elsewhere in Africa, was that education was seen by the people as the means by which one might join the governmental service, which, poorly paying as it might seem to Europeans, offered the comforts and security of a desk job when the only alternative was working the land by the sweat of one's brow without any guarantee of a return. This was the main, and often the only, reason that education was so highly valued.

With independence, opportunities not only for advancement in the bureaucratic hierarchy, but for peculation, increased greatly. In Tanzania, remaining a mere producer from the land became a sign of scholastic failure and even stupidity. Any child of ability got a job in government or job paid by government. Reaching a position in the hierarchy from which it was possible to obstruct the efforts of others unless bribed was therefore the aim of almost every educated person. Once you were 'on seat' your fortune, relatively speaking, was made.[81]

It follows from this that increasing the number of educated people is not necessarily desirable from the economic point of view. It means, on the contrary, that a larger economic surplus has to be extracted from a smaller economic base, for positions in the administration have to be found for the educated people.[82]

Of course, where a government, such as Nyerere's, pursues policies that are designed to extinguish all layers of society between peasant and government, on the grounds that they are intrinsically exploitative (whereas government acts in the common interest), the ill-effects of education are even worse.

Equatorial Guinea is on the other side of the continent. It was the only Spanish colony in Black Africa, and by the time of its independence in 1968 it was one of the richest countries *per capita* on the continent. More to the point it had a level of literacy that was higher than that of the metropole itself, which was still under the rule of the Generalissimo. Under pressure from the United Nations, the first president, Macias Nguema, was democratically elected.

Did everything go swimmingly in Equatorial Guinea as a result of its high level of education? Alas, no. Macias Nguema turned out to be a paranoid maniac. Less educated than many of his compatriots, he felt somewhat sensitive on this point. By the end of his rule eleven years later, by which time a third of the population had either been killed or fled the country, it was dangerous to possess so much as a single page of printed matter, and people who wore spectacles had been eliminated as intellectuals and therefore as potential subverters or mockers of the rule of the Unique Miracle, to use the title he conferred upon himself.

Among the miracles the Unique Miracle performed was a complete collapse of production, despite (or is it because of?) the reintroduction of forced labour into Equatorial Guinea. By the time of his departure from power, executed by his nephew who remains President to this day, production of the country's staple export, cocoa, had declined by 95 per cent. Electricity had become a distant memory, and the national treasury was kept under the President's bed.

It is a common reproach to Belgian colonialism that at the time of the Congo's independence in 1960, there were only a dozen or so Congolese graduates. But now that there are thousands of such graduates, it cannot be said that things have gone a great deal better as a result; and the fate of Sierra Leone, with a long history of educational effort and achievement, does not fortify one's faith in the role of education as the motor of economic advancement.

Still, two arguments remain that might save the day for education. The first is that it is a good in itself. Teaching people who are illiterate to read, for example, gives the potential access to a great deal that would otherwise be unavailable to them.

This ignores the fact that regimes that have been enthusiastic about literacy have also usually been enthusiastic about censorship and ensuring that everyone thinks the same thoughts, or at least expresses the same thoughts. In the modern world, literacy has as often been the instrument of dictatorship as of liberty.

In any case, the argument that education is a good in itself is quite a different one from the argument that education leads to a reduction in poverty, which is that upon which Mr Brown relied to obtain a reputation for 'caring' deeply about the fate of Africa, and therefore of being a compassionate man — compassion being measured by the amount of other people's money you are prepared to pay for the supposed resolution of a social problem.

There is one further possible argument in favour of education as a motor of African economic development. Granted that education is clearly not a sufficient condition for such development, perhaps it is a necessary one. Two examples are instructive here, those of India and Ireland. These two countries for long adopted policies that were inimical to economic growth, the first a debased Gandhian socialism and the second a nationalism that valued autarchy and self-sufficiency above everything else. However, both invested heavily in education and so, when finally they adopted economic policies that promoted economic growth, they were in an excellent position to take advantage of them.

There is no doubt something in this, but several points need to be made. The first is that the two countries were already at very different levels of development from most African countries, in the sense that they already possessed highly sophisticated education institutions, and — in the case of India — industries. Therefore the cases are not strictly comparable. Second, the educational efforts that these countries made were indigenous, which is to say that they did not require outside funding by fairy-godfathers such as Mr Brown (and India's *per capita* income was no higher than sub-Saharan Africa's). And third, most important of all, Peter Bauer showed in his studies of West African and Malayan peasants that, though by no means educated, they were capable of responding to economic incentives and, uneducated as they might have been, were perfectly able to make sensible decisions about investment and savings. In other words, the reason that peasant coffee growers in Tanzania pulled up their bushes and decided to grow maize and other staples for themselves was not because they were stupid or illiterate, or ignorant of their own best interests, but because they knew that if they continued to grow coffee on their land they would be paid (if they were paid at all) in money that would buy them nothing and they would go hungry.

In other words, a consideration of the evidence suggests that an educated population is neither necessary nor sufficient for economic development in Africa, at least at the moment. What is necessary is opportunity and access to markets, for neither of which is primary, secondary or tertiary education a substitute. It is true that at a later stage of development, a more educated and trained population will become necessary: but there is no reason to suppose that a developing society cannot adapt its educational system to its needs. In African circumstances, an educated population ought to be the consequence, not the cause of development.

Just because a man's manner is serious to the point of dourness does not mean that he is incapable of sentimentality. Indeed, his very dourness may be caused by or be a manifestation of his sentimentality. He sees misery everywhere and believes that its principal cause is injustice, which it is his bounden duty to put right; all other activities, including and especially pleasurable ones, are deemed morally frivolous until there is no injustice left.

But there is a great deal that is unattractive, as well as preposterous, in all this. It is earnest without being serious. It is, of course, grossly sentimental: for it involves the pretence that one feels deeply, and equally, for hundreds of millions and even billions of people, no matter how far removed from one they are. It is a mixture of humbug, grandiosity and condescension. It is humbug because one knows that at the first brush with expediency, it will disappear as the blush of a grape to the touch; it is grandiose because of its assumption that redemptive powers are within one's grasp; and it is condescending because it supposes that the supposed beneficiaries of one's largesse are incapable of improving their lives by their own efforts.

In a famous passage in his *Theory of Moral Sentiments*, Adam Smith, who is by no means the apostle of raw selfishness that he is sometimes taken to be, draws our attention to certain human realities:

Let us suppose that the great empire of China, with all its myriads of inhabitants, was suddenly swallowed up by an earthquake, and let us consider how a man of humanity in Europe, who had no sort of connexion with that part of the world, would be affected upon receiving intelligence of this dreadful calamity. He would, I imagine, first of all, express very strongly his sorrow for the misfortune of that unhappy people, he would make many melancholy reflections upon the precariousness of human life, and the vanity of all the labours of man, which could be thus annihilated in a moment. He would too, perhaps, if he was a man of speculation, enter into many reasonings concerning the effects which this disaster might produce upon the commerce of Europe, and the trade and business of the world in general. And when all this fine philosophy was over, when all these fine human sentiments had been once fairly expressed, he would pursue his business or pleasure, take his repose or diversion, with the same ease and tranquillity, as if no such accident had happened. The most frivolous accident that could befall himself would occasion a more real disturbance. If he was to lose his little finger to-morrow, he would not sleep tonight; but, provided he never saw them he would snore with the most profound security over the ruin of a hundred millions of his brethren, and the destruction of that immense multitude seems plainly an object less interesting to him, than this paltry misfortune of his own.

Smith is here drawing our attention, in the most elegant prose, to a fact of human psychology, that what affects us directly is inevitably much more important to us than what happens to other people, no matter how numerous they may be, at a distance. We have the proof of the truth of what he says every day when we read our newspapers. For example, on the day on which I wrote the previous three pages, I learnt that scores, perhaps hundreds, of people had been killed in an explosion in a hotel in Pakistan. I regretted it, of course, and was briefly horrified by the pictures of bodies being removed from the burning ruins; but it didn't affect my appetite for breakfast, let alone for lunch.

It is true that Smith goes on to say that a man who, by losing his little finger, could avert the disaster befalling the hundred millions, and yet does not do so on the grounds of his own self-interest, would be considered a monster of selfishness; and that men, endowed by nature with a sympathy for other men,[83] naturally take an interest in the affairs of others that is independent of their own advantage. But of course the example that he gives, that of a man sacrificing his little finger to avert an earthquake in China, raises the question of whether it is conceivable that such a sacrifice would or could, as a matter of fact, have that result. And this is a question that has to be settled by an appeal to reason and evidence, not to feeling. No amount of emotion will settle the question.

When it comes to the kind of aid to Africa that Mr Brown and others like him propose, then, the question is not whether it would be desirable in the abstract for Africans to be less prone to endemic and epidemic diseases, more educated and less poor than they are, but first whether Mr Brown *et al.* have any moral responsibility to bring about those desired ends, and second whether they have in fact the ability to do so. Everyone knows that power without responsibility is a bad thing, but it is seldom noticed that responsibility without power cannot exist.[84]

It is seldom noticed that there is, in fact, an extremely strong moral resumption against the kind of aid that

Messrs Brown *et al.* propose, namely that it is coercive of the people who pay for it. They have no choice but to pay their taxes; and the coercion is all the worse because they have the freedom, if they so chose, to contribute money to African causes. Indeed, it is highly likely, given the notoriously inefficient manner in which governments spend money, that such individual contributors would do more good than do government subventions, because the contributors would be more likely to take a direct an personal interest in obtaining the most benefit for their money. This, as we shall see, is not the only problem with government assistance.

It might be objected that Mr Brown, while the head of an elected government, had the legal right to levy taxes on the whole population to pursue his moral enthusiasms: after all, he was the head of the party that was elected to power.

Of the legal and constitutional right there can be little doubt, but that does not settle the matter of the moral right. First, in modern political conditions, parties are generally elected to power by a minority, sometimes a small minority, of the adult population. The majority's consent to any particular measure cannot therefore be assumed. Second, any party's programme is an amalgam of proposed measures and policies; in making a choice between parties, the elector takes an overall view. His choice of one party over another cannot be taken to mean approval of or consent to every last proposal down to the fine print — and aid to Africa, if it is included in a party's political programme at all, is not likely to be a major consideration of the voters in a country distant from Africa, and with many difficult problems of its own.

Third, even if it were true that the majority of the population were strongly in favour of its government giving aid to Africa, this would not justify coercion of the rest of the population. The majority does not have unlimited sovereignty over the property of everyone; and the election of a head of government in a country such as Britain is not, our ought not to be, the election of a dictator *pro tempore*. In coercing money from the entire population to do good works, Mr Brown (and, to be fair to him, he is no different in this from all his predecessors) is acting as a dictator, pure and simple. His dour sentimentality led him to suppose that he had a duty to save the Africans; and his constitutional position led him to suppose that he had a right to dispose of everyone's money as he saw fit. Sentimentality, then, is a prop to, if it does not originate, his tendency to coercion: a coercion that is mild, no doubt, and lost in a thousand other little coercions, but is not the less coercion for all that.

The presumption, then, must be against government aid (if it is accepted that needless coercion is something that ought to be avoided). The only thing that could justify coercion in this matter is if the government could be said to have an indubitable moral duty towards Africa.

Where could such a duty come from? There are two possible sources, the first historical and economic and the second from a general ethical principle.

The historical and economic source of the duty derives from the question 'Where does Africa's poverty come from?' *Prima facie*, this is a very strange question, for poverty is man's natural condition and it is wealth that always needs to be explained. Perhaps the question would be better expressed as 'Why does Africa's poverty persist, despite the potential for development?'

Two favoured answers are given to this question that supposedly entail a country like Britain's inescapable moral duty to provide aid. The first is the Atlantic slave trade and colonialism, and the second is the world economic system.

The slave trade could not have been carried out without widespread African co-operation. Until the mass production of the anti-malarial quinine (which did not occur until well after the slave trade was suppressed), Europeans were quite unable in any numbers to penetrate the African interior. The supply of slaves came from purely African sources. No doubt the European slavers benefited more from the trade, economically-speaking, than African slavers; but that was because they came from an infinitely more sophisticated material and intellectual culture in the first place. It was not a moral difference. The fact remains that if there had been no African slavers, there would have been no Atlantic slave trade, at least on anything like the scale approaching that on which it was actually carried out.

Many developed societies have experienced catastrophes that, while not the same as that of the slave trade, were as great, and have yet recovered to the pitch of prosperity. Furthermore, the very large parts of Africa that did not experience the Atlantic slave trade have developed no further than those that did (though some of them, it is true, did experience the Arab slave trade).

As to colonialism in Africa, there can be no doubt that, especially in the earlier phases of its short career, it was responsible for brutality and sometimes devastation. But by the time it receded, its record (from the point of view of economic development) was distinctly more nuanced. At Ghana's independence, for example, the country had large foreign reserves and a prospering export sector. It was richer, *per capita*, than South Korea. The almost immediate dissipation of its wealth was not in any direct sense the consequence of colonialism, though it might be argued that the mind-set that produced the dissipation was a consequence of colonialism. However, the moral argument for independence was that the population and leaders of the country had the right to self-determination because they were not moral or political minors. This being so, they, and not the colonialists, were responsible for the disasters that subsequently befell them.

In assessing the material effects of an historical process such as colonialism, it is necessary to balance the harms done against the possible benefits received (the backwardness of Africa being such that the wheel and writing were unknown in large parts of it, and all transport was by human porterage or by canoe). Counterfactual speculation — what Africa would have been like if there had been no colonialism — is... well, extremely speculative. The assessment is necessarily a highly complex one, even without taking into consideration intangibles such as cultural damage done, and no definitive answer is likely ever to be reached.[85] As to the responsibility of people now living for an era that ended nearly half a century ago, this too is a complex question. It might be argued that, if their current prosperity were built on the back of colonialism, as it were, they owe some kind of reparations to Africa, if current African poverty were the consequence of the colonialism that made them, the Europeans, rich. But the overall effect of African colonialism on European economic development is itself a matter of dispute, whether ultimately it enriched or impoverished. No one in his right mind would suggest, if it emerged that Africa benefited from colonialism at European expense, that Africans owed anything to Europeans.

From this it is clear that sentimentality is not a proper approach to the matter, and no appeal to selected pictures of undernourished African children a substitute for thought.

Nor is the fact that aid, a very word that sometimes makes opposition to it difficult (for who can be against assistance to the needy?), is intended to help some of the poorest people in the world sufficient warrant that it does actually have that effect. Tanzania grew progressively poorer as it received the highest *per capita* aid allocation on the continent. Oil revenues in Nigeria, which is analogous to aid in that it is unearned money flowing into the country from outside, has probably had a harmful effect overall. It has encouraged the importation of food to the detriment of local farmers, still the majority of the population; it has sharpened political and ethnic competition for power, whose major prize is control of the oil revenues, the overwhelming source of foreign currency in Nigeria (as was aid in Nyerere's Tanzania). This explains, incidentally, why those countries in Africa extravagantly endowed with natural resources have done no better, and in many instances worse, than those countries without.

African leaders have long realised the truth of the sixteenth-century German bishop's dictum, that the poor are a goldmine. Like the nineteenth century President of Paraguay, Carlos Antonio Lopez, who so loved his country that he owned half of it, African leaders so love the poor that they have resolved to maintain them in their poverty. Easily able to capture the lion's share of the aid that is given to their countries on the pretext that they are so poor, African elites have realised that there is wealth to be made from poverty. And thus it comes about that much aid to Africa is of more use to the real estate markets of European capitals and resorts than to African peasants. It is also a form of outdoor relief to those Europeans who want to do good to the African continent, but at other people's expense, and often at a decent salary with generous living expenses. Certainly, there is not a single case of an African country transformed for the better by foreign aid, and those African countries that have enjoyed good economic growth (which is not quite the same thing as reduction of poverty, of course, but is a precondition of it) recently have not done so because of such aid.

There is considerable evidence that foreign aid has funded civil wars in Africa, or at least the continuation of them.

So aid is neither sufficient nor necessary for Africa to escape from its poverty. What then remains of its supposed justification, argued for with such dour compassion by Mr Brown?

We are left, I think, with Singerian moral universalism, which is the grossest of sentimentality with all the fun taken out. Peter Singer is a strict utilitarian who believes in the felicific calculus: that to behave ethically one's actions must be calculated to bring about the maximum of pleasure and the minimum of pain. Since everyone is to count equally, it does not matter whose pain is maximised and whose pain is minimised. Given the choice between pleasing his son with a small gift that he does not need, and saving the sight of a little boy with antibiotic ointment eight thousands miles away, it is clear what the decent parent ought to do. He should ignore his own son.

This is all preposterous, psychologically, theoretically and practically. Surely there is no one in the world who has no partiality for the people whom he knows and likes, as compared to those whom he either dislikes or are completely unknown to him. Moreover, if there were such a person, we should consider him at the best to be mentally ill, as suffering from a peculiar form of Asperger's syndrome, and at the worst to be a monster of inhumanity. Who would pass an injured person in the street, or refuse to treat him, on the grounds that the money spent on saving his life would actually save more lives if applied elsewhere in the world?

It is hardly a new observation that people who are concerned with humanity in general are often not much concerned for people in particular. Rousseau famously said that he knew mankind, but not men; his sentimental doctrines led in fairly short order to ideological massacre. Lenin was a man with a burning love of humanity in general, and a hatred for almost all individual manifestations of it, with consequences that are by now sufficiently well-known.

Nor is it altogether surprising that Professor Singer, who makes universal benevolence the touchstone of his philosophy, ends up by advocating, on ethical grounds, the killing of fairly large numbers of human beings as either too wretched or too expensive to maintain in life (his own practice has been, of course, famously different). A man who became famous by advocating rights for animals ends up by arguing for policies that, in Nazi Germany, turned out to be a dry run for the Holocaust.[86]

While it is fairly easy to be sure of the beneficial consequences of helping an old lady across the road, it is rather more difficult to assess the beneficial consequences of giving money to a large charity such as, say, Oxfam.[87]

The more grandiose the target, the less sure the aim.

This means that nothing is sure about Mr Brown's policy but the sentimentality behind it, a combination of condescension (the assumption that Africans left to themselves cannot, even in theory, solve their own problems), self-importance (that Mr Brown has a unique duty in their regard), and self-indulgence (the warm glow inside probably given him by the knowledge that he is a compassionate politician, indeed more-compassionate-than-thou). This is frivolity, though without gaiety.

One is reminded of what Rousseau wrote in *The Creed of a Savoyard Priest*. 'If I am mistaken, I am honestly mistaken, and therefore my error will not be counted to me as a crime.' No, it will never be counted as a crime, because what is important above all is the psychological cuddliness of the principles upon which a man claims to act.

Conclusion

'... a sentimentalist is simply one who desires to have the luxury of an emotion without paying for it.'

Oscar Wilde

Sentimentality does no harm when it is confined to the private sphere. No one, surely, is entirely immune from having his emotions manipulated by a saccharine story, picture or piece of music.

But as the wellspring of public policy, or of public reaction to events or social problems, it is as disastrous as it is prevalent. There is a great deal of sentimentality in the modern idea of multiculturalism, which supposes that all aspects of all cultures are mutually compatible and can coexist as easily as restaurants of varying cuisines in the centre of a cosmopolitan city, simply because mankind is fundamentally, always and everywhere, prompted by, or susceptible to, expressions of goodwill. The fact that many multicultural societies are riven by hostility, even after hundreds of years, or that it is not altogether easy to reconcile western ideas of freedom with the death sentence for apostates that all four Sunni schools of legal interpretation advocate, as well as with many other precepts of Islamic law, slips away from the mind of multiculturalists as an eel is likely to slip through the hands of someone trying to catch one manually. If you ask a multiculturalist what, for example, Somalis have brought to a country like Britain *qua* Somalis,[88] he is likely to remain silent. He can hardly suggest that it is their political tradition (which is what caused them to flee Somalia in the first place) that he values; he knows nothing of their literature, or even if there is any; of their art and architecture he will likewise know nothing; he will be vaguely aware that the Somali contribution to modern science is nil; he has not examined their customs, many of which he would probably find repellent if he did examine them; and he will probably be unable even to name a single traditional Somali dish, an unusual degree of ignorance and indifference even for a multiculturalist. (The way to a multiculturalist's heart is definitely through his stomach.)

And yet he will persist in stating, with almost the religious certainty of one who accepts the carbon dioxide theory of global warming, that the presence of enclaves of Somalis, maintaining their own culture within those enclaves, is indisputably and by definition an enrichment to British, or to any western society, as if life were best lived as an exhibit in a vast anthropological museum.

None of this is meant to imply that the advent of immigrants or foreigners cannot enrich a recipient culture enormously: the influx of Huguenot or Austrian and German Jewish refugees to Britain are obvious cases in point. And it is undoubtedly true that the influx of foreigners of many different lands has improved the quality of the available food in Britain beyond all recognition. But it is another thing entirely to argue that massive immigration is a good in itself precisely because of the ethnic and cultural diversity it brings to a small space, and because mankind is one big happy family. That sort of idea, or rather feeling, is the kind of sentimentality that an alcoholic drink imparts to the mind after a hard day at work: that life is really rather good after all, that all men are brothers, and that the situation, though disastrous, will work out well in the end. Needless to say, it is no substitute for genuine thought.

But in field after field, sentimentality has triumphed. It has blighted the lives of millions of children, creating a dialectic of overindulgence and neglect. It has destroyed educational standards and caused untold emotional instability because of the theory of human relations it has espoused. Sentimentality has been the forerunner and accomplice of brutality wherever the policies suggested by it have been put into place.[89] The cult of feeling destroys the ability to think, or even the awareness that it is necessary to think. Pascal was absolutely right when he said:

Travaillons donc à bien penser. Voilà le principe de la morale.

Let us labour, therefore, to think well. That is the principle of morality.

Notes

1   That the effect is considerable and important is suggested by the following anecdote from the prison in which I worked. A young man of Pakistani origin who was imprisoned for a comparatively minor offence came to see me because of an alleged problem in his stomach. I quickly realised that his real problem was anxiety or, as it turned out, fear. Not very long before, he had acted as a prosecution witness in the 'honour-killing' of a young woman by her father and brother. The other prisoners of Pakistani origin — for some reason growing quickly more numerous — ganged up on him and had threatened to attack him for his disloyalty his group and to the system of forced marriage, which is highly convenient and agreeable for such young men. This was not a manifestation of prisoners' normal solidarity, according to which there is no lower form of life than an informer (unless it be a sex criminal). Prisoners draw the line at murder, at least murder not committed in the pursuit of other criminal ends such as bank robbery, and willingly testify in such cases. It was specifically for his implicit threat to the system of forced marriage that my patient was being persecuted. I asked for him to be transferred immediately to a distant prison where he

would not be known. His abdominal discomfort ceased at once.

2   The infant mortality rate in the borough in the East End of London in which my father was born in 1909 was 124 per 1000 live births. That is to say, an eighth of all children born alive died before their first birthday. His life expectancy at birth was 49 years. Survivors of that first perilous year had a life expectancy of only about 55.

3   This would not have been a bad fiction — mankind often has to live *as if*, that is to say as if something that is not true, or at least unprovable, were true — if it had led to the search for and fostering of talent. Of course, it did no such thing.

4   Here I am indebted to a short book, *Spoil the Child*, by Lucie Street, Phoenix House, published in 1961. This book is short, alarming, illuminating and hilarious.

5   If there has been a general ascent of the population into the middle class, it explains how there can have been a rise and fall of general educational standards at the same time, the effect of social ascension having overcome that of educational deterioration. It also helps to explain why the rate of social mobility may well have declined, the middle classes being able better to protect their children from the effects of ludicrous educational ideas, thus turning a class society into a caste society.

6   As Skimpole put it, 'I only ask to be free. The butterflies are free. Mankind will surely not deny to Harold Skimpole what it concedes to the butterflies!'

7   C-l-e-a-n, clean, verb active, to make bright, to scour. W-i-n, win, d-e-r, der, winder, a casement. When a boy knows this out of the book, he goes and does it. Thus Mr Squeers in *Nicholas Nickleby*.

8   The really hard line sentimentalist and romantic would deny that there were any to give.

9   In 1954, the Ministry of Education's *Bulletin for Primary Schools* said 'The curriculum is to be thought of in terms of activity and experience rather than knowledge to be acquired and facts to be

stored.'

10 Now what I want is facts… Facts alone are wanted in life.

11 *Education through Experience in the Infant School Years*, 1950

12 Political correctness is often the attempt to make sentimentality socially obligatory or legally enforceable.

13 The possession of an army and navy implies, paradoxically for someone who claims that all forms of language are equal, that a standard language is inferior to all the other forms of that language, at least morally, in so far as it resorts to force to impose itself on the population. Thus anyone who, for example, teaches a child in a slum to speak and write a standard language is oppressing him. Certainly, this idea can make life much easier for teachers, at least in the short run.

14 Professor Pinker omits to mention that this is true of many subjects. Many of the things I learnt at medical school turned out, on further investigation, not to have been true. This does not mean that they should not have been taught.

15 Though biological, they also have an important social or educational aspect. No group of people, so far as I know, fails to train its children in the acceptable way to dispose of urine and faeces; and if it were to exist, I should not wish to encounter it.

16 I have a suspicion also, though I cannot prove it, that qualities such as the ability to concentrate are a little like the acquisition of language; if they are not learnt by a certain age, they are never learnt.

17 As yet not to surgery. I don't think anyone would subject himself to an operation by a surgeon who had been educated along these lines. And in fairness, it is not quite true that no art history is ever taught to art students. I met one who was just entering her second year of study of this subject. I asked her what she had done in her first year. 'African art,' she replied. And the second? 'Roy Liechtenstein,' she said. As Pudd'nhead Wilson put it, 'It's better to know nothing than to know what ain't so.'

18 And Britain, for some reason that I cannot understand, and

alas for other countries, is a vanguard nation. Look on Britain, o ye mighty, and despair!

[19] Among my mother's papers that I found after her death, I found the report of a private detective who sought evidence of my father's adultery, which was then one of the few grounds of divorce. He did not find it; from what I have heard, he must have been incompetent.

[20] It is not only in the Anglo-Saxon world that this desire existed. In August, 2008, *Le Monde* carried an obituary of a writer called Tony Duvert. Duvert's great idea was that the state should have nothing to do with sexual relations. There should be no laws or enforceable contracts in such matters. Presumably no sexual desires, not even those of a Jeffrey Dahmer, should be outlawed. Referring to his novel *Paysage de fantaisie*, which was awarded the Medicis prize in 1973, the obituary says: 'In a temporary children's home, the inmates could abandon themselves to all their whims of the moment, without any taboo, any disapproving look, without reproach. There is in the book a sort of celebration of amorality, of a ferocious joy. And in the overturning of grammar [with which it is written] … a challenge is thrown to all literary and ethical conventions. But,' continues the obituary, 'it is in *Journal d'un innocent* that is expressed even more clearly this pagan innocence. In a world without necessity or suffering, somewhere in the South, sexual couplings succeed one another with a total and absolute unselfconsciousness.' This is surely pure adolescent sentimental drivel. Perhaps not coincidentally, the obituary begins, 'The writer Tony Duvert, aged 63, was found dead on 20 August, at home, in the little village of Thore-la-Rochelle. His death occurred a month before.' False sentiment leading to real tragedy.

[21] And also a religious person, or at least some religious people, who know that 'My kingdom in not of this world,' but not many secular utopians.

[22] A considerably larger proportion of British children have a television in their bedrooms (79per cent) than have a biological

father living at home with them.

23 When I was about eight, my mother left my father for a short period and she took my brother and I to live in an hotel. To distract my attention from the change of circumstances, she bought me *The Observer's Book of Butterflies* and *The Observer's Book of Aeroplanes*. I am still quite good at recognising the aircraft of the 1950s.

24 The sociobiologists argue that the reason for the increased violence of step-parents is that step-children represent competition for the resources that might otherwise be available for their genetic offspring. This seems to me to be ludicrously reductive. If step-parents are many times more likely to be violent to children than biological parents, the fact remains that most of them are not violent.

25 I have several times overheard young Britons discussing the night before and saying that they had an incomparable time. The evidence for this was that, thanks to the amount of alcohol they had drunk, they could remember nothing at all about it. This seems to indicate a rather pessimistic view of the possibilities of human social intercourse. The number of words the English language (as used in England) now has for being drunk — bladdered, wasted, hammered etc. — reminds one of the number of words the Eskimos allegedly had for snow.

26 One of the manifestations of this belief is the refusal of men and women to make a commitment to one another — a complaint one can overhear on buses and trains all the time. The person who refuses to make a commitment refuses to foreclose on any possibilities that may arise later in his life and of which he might want to take advantage. He thinks of freedom as an infinite range of possibilities: an infinite range meaning that none is foreclosed by a decision already taken. He does not realise that every course of action has advantages and disadvantages, conveniences and inconveniences; that a perfect existence without remainder of frustration, loss and unhappiness is not

possible, is a chimera.

27 The confusion is not merely verbal. The notion that anyone having anything to do with children, either in a professional or amateur capacity, is likely to be a paedophile has become officially enshrined and has led, as ever, to a bureaucratic industry of administrative obstruction and compulsory checks. Guilt is presumed and innocence must be proved. In the meantime, routine sexual abuse of children continues unabated.

28 There was a connection between lynching and sentimentality even in the southern United States. White womanhood was placed on an altar at which the sentimental, who no doubt often behaved in a less than chivalrous fashion when confronted by an individual of the species in the proximity of home, might worship.

29 Here the newspaper may actually be understating its own case, though I think for devious reasons. The 64 per cent refers to the re-conviction, not the re-offending, rate; and since the clear-up rate of all reported crimes is 5.5 per cent, it is fair to assume that the real rate of re-offending after release from prison is, if the released prisoners are averagely competent criminals chased by averagely incompetent policemen (which, of course, they might not be), closer to 100 per cent than to 64 per cent. This conclusion is strengthened further by the fact that many crimes, perhaps a half, go unreported, and that the clear-up rate is exaggerated by statistical legerdemain on the part of the police. But the abysmally low clear-up rate is not in concert with the emotional tone of the newspaper's message, which is why it sticks to the re-offending i.e. reconviction rate of 'only' 64 per cent. For re-offending read re-conviction, a very different matter.

30 For a fuller discussion of this matter, see my *Junk Medicine: Pharmacological Lies and the Addiction Bureaucracy*, Harriman House, 2007

31 I owe this formulation to Mr Myron Magnet, of New York.

32 The theory on which probation now operates is entirely

sentimental, though it was realistic when probation was introduced. Originally, probation was an alternative to imprisonment for first offenders who were frightened of being imprisoned. It was persuasion and an appeal to reason, backed up by a credible sanction if that appeal did not work. However, probation came to be seen as a sanction in itself, even for people who had amply demonstrated by their previous conduct that they had no intention of listening to such an appeal. It was used merely to keep the prison population down. The supposition that people who had committed myriad offences would cease committing them merely because they visited a decent man or woman in an office once a week or a fortnight for fifteen minutes makes the novels published by Mills and Boon seem like works of coal-face social realism. The causes of criminality, we are often told by criminologists, are so complex than no normal human mind can comprehend them; but it seems to me likely that one of the causes at least is a lack of serious consequences of criminal behaviour.

33 Actually, it should really be innocence by association. Linda Chamberlain was an Australian mother of three, including a baby only a few months old who went missing on an outing in the outback in 1980 (see discussion in the text). The mother went to the police and told them that a dingo must have taken the baby while she looked away. Her unemotional demeanour made a bad impression on the police and later on the public. How could any mother who had lost a baby and had not killed it herself remain so cool? She was therefore charged with murder and convicted on flimsy circumstantial and forensic evidence. She served four years in prison until the forensic evidence was thoroughly discredited, and she was both released and compensated. Recently, a man who claimed to have been out hunting dingoes at the time of the baby's disappearance said that he saw a dingo with a baby in its mouth. Be that as it may, had Linda Chamberlain sobbed a little more at the time, she might have avoided prison altogether.

Incidentally, the same author later animadverted on the fact that Mrs McCann cried in public when she embraced her other two children before going on one of her trips. She quoted (with obvious agreement) an acquaintance of Mrs McCann who demanded to know 'Is nothing private any more?'

34 Plath's tendency to extravagant self-pity and dramatisation of her woes is illustrated also by what she wrote after a friend had borrowed a book from her, which she herself had already disfigured with underlinings in ink, which he marked in a few additional places with a pencil. When he returned the book, she wrote to her mother 'I was furious, feeling my children had been raped, or beaten, by an alien'. Only someone deeply self-absorbed could write in this vein.

35 Currently, the ratio in Britain is about 30 attempts to one completed suicide. In Plath's time, the ratio might have been quite a lot lower, but still substantial.

36 Plath, as a woman, was a victim ex officio, at least on the world-view that was to develop within a few years of her death. The blurb for a book by Jean Rhys that I found at the back of a Penguin paperback encapsulated it well. 'Jean Rhys wrote about women — society's victims — with all the passion and despair of a loser.' There could hardly be any greater incitement to uncritical feminine self-pity, unless, of course, it be Virginia Woolf's *Three Guineas*, in which privilege brazenly masquerades as impotent impoverishment.

37 I am not by a long way the first to object to her use of the Holocaust in connection with her own personal drama. George Steiner asked whether 'any of us have license to locate our personal disasters, raw as these may be, in Auschwitz?' Seamus Heaney wrote 'however [the] violence and vindictiveness [of the poem 'Daddy'] can be understood or excused in light of the poet's parental and marital relations, [it] rampages so permissively in the history of other people's sorrows that it simply overdraws its rights to our sympathy.' As for the personal disasters to which

Steiner alludes, Janet Malcolm, in her book on the relationship between Sylvia Plath and Ted Hughes, tells us that she, having been nearly contemporaneous with Plath, shared her problems of growing up middle class female with literary leanings and ambitions in America in the 1950s. Because of the still-existent cult of respectability, 'We lied to our parents, and we lied to each other and we lied to ourselves, so addicted to deception had we become. We were an uneasy, shifty-eyed generation.' So now, after the liberation of the 1960s, everyone always tells the truth to his parents, to each other and to himself? Even if true, this account of the travails of young Americans growing up middle class in the 1950s hardly invited comparison with the Holocaust. I don't think a deep acquaintance with Holocaust literature would be needed to establish this point.

[38] Whose psychological doppelganger, as it were, is self-esteem, into which, indeed, it is liable, with the right persuasion, or indoctrination, to transform itself.

[39] I am indebted for my account to *The Wilkomirski Affair: A Study in Biographical Truth*, by Stefan Machler, Schocken Books, NY, 2001

[40] I should perhaps here point out that at least some of the elements of her story correspond to things that actually happen, if rarely. I have myself given assistance to the police in the case of parents who abused their own children in such a way that, had I not seen the video film of it that they took in order to sell for large sums of money to people who took pleasure in that kind of thing, I should not have deemed credible if I had merely been told about it by someone else and not seen it with my own eyes, or even possible.

[41] The connection between kitsch and sentimentality on the one hand, and pornography and brutality on the other, could hardly be better illustrated than in these titles.

[42] It is ironic that, not very long after the reality of child abuse was generally accepted, two eminent British paediatricians,

Professor Sir Roy Meadow and Professor David Southall, who did so much to reveal a particular type of it, namely that committed by parents to make their children ill, became victims — dare I use that word? — of a concerted and vengeful campaign to ruin them. So effective was this campaign that, for a time at least, British paediatricians would not testify as experts in court cases involving child abuse.

[43] The Harkis were Algerians who fought on the French side during the Algerian war of independence. It is estimated that 60,000 of them were killed in Algeria immediately after independence. Many thousands of others fled to France, where, however, they were not received as heroes but with shame, and were housed in camps for decades. All of a sudden, in 2001, there was a flurry of books published in France about their fate and ill-treatment.

[44] Though honesty compels me to admit that the victims of assault are often not the cream of humanity themselves.

[45] Her method of coming to terms with herself contrasts interestingly with that of another Belgian immigrant to the United States, Paul de Man. An eminent professor of literature at Yale, he had written ferociously pro-Nazi and anti-Semitic propaganda during the occupation of Belgium. He came to terms with himself by propounding, and gaining widespread academic acceptance of, the post-modernist idea that texts have no fixed or indubitable meaning, and that their interpretation by the reader is all. Thus, words such as 'The Jew is to be exterminated once and for all' might just as well be taken to mean 'The Jew is to be cherished and granted equal rights' as what the naïve and philosophically unsophisticated believer in the meaning of words would take the first statement to mean. De Man was a one man refutation of the notion that the study of literature always makes you a better person.

[46] Nor were they like those Romanians who, during the late dictator Ceausescu's baleful rule, claimed to be Jewish,

notwithstanding one of the most powerful popular traditions of anti-Semitism in the world. No; they simply wanted to be allowed to emigrate to Israel. If Ceausescu had allowed emigration to Paraguay instead of Israel, they would gladly have claimed to be Guarani Indians.

[47] What would we think of a doctor who heard Mrs Gradgrind say 'I think there is a pain somewhere in the room, but I cannot positively say that I have got it,' and proceeded to treat people in the room at random for that pain, without expressing an interest in who precisely had it? For the equivocations of Rogoberta Menchu, see David Stoll, *Rogoberta Menchu and the Story of All Poor Guatemalans*, Westview, 1999. There is much evidence that Menchu was manipulated by her French amanuensis, the anthropologist Elisabeth Burgos-Debray, who wanted a straightforward story of good and evil in order to drum up foreign support for the revolutionary movement.

[48] In all this there is the romantic assumption that the cruel, violent and unpleasant are more real and above all authentic that the kind, peaceful and delightful. This, in the first chapter of her book, 'Margaret B. Jones' witnesses the shooting of her drug boss, called Kraziak,. 'Blood bubbled out of his mouth and neck and he gasped, trying to breathe... He moaned..., the sound pushing blood out of his neck and mouth.' In the second chapter, we learn about how she was sexually abused aged six. 'I had blood running down my legs.' In the same chapter, we learn how cruelly she was then treated by some foster parents. 'One family ate together each night, not allowing any of their foster kids to join them. After they had had their fill they would leave the table and allow us to eat the leftovers off their dirty plates.' Here we see the sentimentality of Oliver Twist asking for more combined, and intimately linked, with the salacity of Hannibal Lecter. It is not that any of the things she described was intrinsically impossible: indeed, much worse things happen regularly, and after the Twentieth Century one dare not say in any case what is

impossible. Rather, it is the evident desire that she should be thought to have witnessed and suffered these things that is significant, which would confer upon her a moral authority not available to a person of her age who had gone through life, relatively speaking, like a hot knife through butter.

[49] In the prison in which I worked, many prisoners evinced concern for the dogs from whom they were separated by imprisonment. I am a dog-lover myself, and we had many conversations about the consolation of canine companionship. I learned, however, not to ask the breed of dog they had: for it was invariably either a pit bull or a Rottweiler.

[50] Here it must be admitted that Ms Jones' fiction has at least the merit of verisimilitude. In the prison in which I worked, I noticed not only that the great majority of white criminals — and increasingly coloured ones as well, despite the natural disadvantage for this kind of self-adornment that their dark skins conferred upon them — were tattooed, but that quite a number of them were tattooed with the names of their children. In other words, they loved their children sufficiently to have themselves mutilated on their behalf, but not enough to support them financially or in any other way. There could not be a more eloquent testimony to the hollowness and futility of sentimentality. Those prisoners who were so lacking in foresight as to have themselves tattooed also with the name of the mother or mothers of their children often felt obliged later to have a cross tattooed over it or them: this being a cheaper and quicker, though less thorough, method of erasure than laser removal. They never erased the names of their children, even though they often had no contact with them.

[51] In 1988 a British feminist publisher, Virago, published a slender collection of short stories entitled *Down the Road, Worlds Away*. It purported to be by Rahila Khan, a young woman of Pakistani extraction, the daughter of immigrants, and described the psychological and other difficulties of growing up in two very

different cultures in a working class district of a British industrial town. The publishers — correctly, I think — saw literary merit in the collection. They printed and distributed it before having met the author; they were subsequently surprised to discover that Rahila Khan was a pseudonym for the Reverend Toby Forward, a Church of England clergyman, who had surmised, no doubt correctly, that his book would never be published under his own identity. As it happened, he knew what he was talking about because he, unlike the editors at Virago, had grown up in precisely the kind of area and social conditions that the book described; but authenticity, alas, turned out to be a matter of race. Although the book never claimed to be other than a work of fiction, the publishers destroyed the stock still in the warehouse, and recalled all unsold copies from the bookshops, thus turning it into an expensive bibliographical rarity, a copy of which I am glad to say that I possess. The book contains stories about the inner worlds of both young women of Pakistani origin and white working class boys. While it was perfectly acceptable for a woman of Pakistani origin to write about the latter, it was not acceptable for a white man of working class origin to write about the former (that he was a Church of England clergyman was no doubt an added disqualification). This establishes how difficult it is even for the most liberal-minded intelligentsia to escape from racialised ways of thought. In their case, of course, racialised thought tends to the sentimental rather than the brutal, implicitly conferring as it does superior moral authority on one race compared with another. No doubt it is better to be sentimental than brutal: but, as we have seen, the one is often a harbinger of, or but a gestalt switch away, from the other.

[52] Mobutu himself was perfectly aware of the political advantages to be derived from the assumption of victimhood. In order to overcome the effects of a colonial past, and in the name of authenticity, he decreed that all Zairian citizens should abandon their European names to which they had been

accustomed since birth, and take on African ones instead. Likewise, no one was henceforth to wear a collar and tie; instead he had designed a national costume, which again he imposed in the name of authenticity. In this way, he made himself all-important. When he had a toothache, however, he commandeered a jet aircraft of the national airline and flew to Paris for dental treatment.

53 If oppression really conferred superior virtue, there would be something to be said in its favour.

54 I have heard it disputed that they were really the worst. The Mongols, after all, were no mean slaughterers, and a third of the German population died in the Thirty Years' War. In the War of the Triple Alliance, ninety-five per cent of Paraguay's male population expired. But if the massacres of the Twentieth Century were not certainly the worst, they were certainly the best publicised. Not even a semi-educated person could know nothing of them. I think you could probably go quite a long way down an average street in Europe or America before you met anyone who had heard of the War of the Triple Alliance.

55 In his *Theory of Justice*, the late Professor Rawls, much concerned with the fate of the worst-off people in his society, or at least with showing that he was much concerned with the fate of the worst-off people in his society, proposed that unequal social arrangements were just in so far as they tended to the improvement of the condition of those worst-off members of his society. Of course, his principle could be extended to the whole human population of the world. If this is what justice requires, so much the worse for justice: personally, I prefer civilisation as being much the more important desideratum.

56 Primo Levi had a terrible and agonising dream while in Auschwitz that no one would believe him afterwards when he recounted what he had seen and experienced.

57 This is not to deny that the France of the time was in a peculiar situation. It had just emerged from the Algerian War of

Independence in which great crimes had been committed — on both sides, of course. The massacre of nationalists in Algeria carried out on the very day of the ending of the war in Europe was known, or knowable, but unacknowledged. The brutal repression of a revolt in Madagascar in 1947 was likewise unacknowledged. And France was still living in a state of denial about the German Occupation, De Gaulle having carefully fostered the myth of an heroically resisting France betrayed by a traitor, Petain, and a few henchmen. There was considerable censorship exercised in defence of this view. The General himself was not above making mildly anti-Semitic remarks, most notoriously after the Six Days War. But none of this made the France of 1968 remotely like Nazi Germany, or De Gaulle like Hitler.

58 Stephen Lawrence, a young black man, was stabbed to death on 22 April 1993 by five or six white thugs who shouted racist abuse at him and had no obvious motive, other than racial antagonism and a lust for blood, for killing him. That they had knives with them suggests that they were of violent predisposition.

59 Indeed, this definition appears to have already received some official sanction. The report on the death of Stephen Lawrence (p146) criticises particular police officers for not accepting that the murder was of racist inspiration. 'Where any person alleges racist motivation it must have or should have been known to them all that the ACPO [Association of Chief Police Officers] definition required the matter to be dealt with as a racist incident.' Note that the definition allows for no discretion in the matter. It does not say the police must treat an incident that someone claims to be racial as if it 'might be' a racist one, with a consequent requirement to investigate the possibility. Of course, discretion, or the exercise of judgment, can lead to error; but so can lack of discretion. Incidentally, the report on the murder of Stephen Lawrence was not the first official report to treat the beliefs of

members of a group believed to be universally victimised with sentimental reverence. Lord Scarman, in his report on the Brixton riots in 1981, said that, as far as the widespread belief of blacks in Brixton that the police unfairly harassed them was concerned, 'Whether justified or not... the belief here is as important as the fact.' For reasons of sentimentality, the report makes no attempt to distinguish between, on the one hand, the undoubted truth that beliefs, whether true or false, are sociologically important, as motives for men's actions; and on the other hand the fact that beliefs in themselves are true or false, justified or unjustified, in so far as they correspond to reality. It is surely a matter of considerable intellectual, moral, social and practical importance whether the beliefs in question were true of false, justified or unjustified. The fact that a senior lawyer could have taken so little interest in the question of the truth of the beliefs, simply because, even if false, they had a considerable influence on men's conduct, is curious. What would we say of a court that found a man guilty simply because some people strongly believed that he was guilty? Lord Scarman was surely led astray by sentimentality. He devoted many paragraphs in his report to the bad social conditions which many of the rioters had endured; to have reproached them afterwards with irrational beliefs would have seemed like kicking men when they were down, so he avoided the question completely. On Lord Scarman's principles, or lack of them, it would not matter, incidentally, whether Binjamin Wilkomirski never left Switzerland during the war, so long as he believed that he had, the belief being as important as the fact. It is perhaps hardly surprising that fraudulent accounts of suffering should receive so favourable a reception in the world when even eminent lawyers are indifferent to the truth or otherwise of the beliefs upon which people act, or say they act.

60 The use of the term black in contradistinction to white also propagates the view that both black and white are entirely uniform as within their groups and opposed as between them. On

this view, a successful lawyer of Ghanaian descent has more in common with a drug-dealer of Jamaican descent than with a successful white lawyer, who himself has more in common with a schizophrenic tramp than with the lawyer of Ghanaian descent. This view is possible only for out-and-out racists, or those who view blacks as victims ex officio, as it were, and whites as victimisers. This, of course, is grossly sentimental.

61 They may even be super-totalitarian. Even the Gestapo and the NKVD usually made some attempt, for form's sake, to make the evidence fit the alleged crime. That they did so suggests that they had at least a concept of innocence, even if they never actually employed it in practice. What possible concept of innocence does the report's definition of racial incident allow? The Gestapo, incidentally, saw its duty as not merely or even principally to enforce laws. As Robert Gellately puts it in *The Gestapo and German Society*, p. 12, 'the Gestapo took it upon themselves to enforce not merely laws (or decrees and ordinances), but the far broader range of behaviour thought by them to fall outside the spirit or ideology of the 'new order.'' The report on the murder of Stephen Lawrence suggests compulsory re-education of large numbers of people, whose thoughts must subsequently conform to the 'correct' ones. Among other things, they have to be taught to 'value' cultural diversity. Gellately quotes the research of Reinhard Mann on the Gestapo records of Dusseldorf: a quarter of their files deal with 'non-conforming verbal utterances.'

62 Hence to be against authority, whatever it may be, is to be virtuous. I have heard many patients say that they are opposed to authority, intending it as self-praise.

63 It is literally the case that often they were not permitted to know the exact nature of the allegations that had been made against them, nor who had made them, nor what the evidence in their favour was, before they were asked to rebut them. It was as if Kafka's *The Trial* had not been taken as a warning, but as a

model.

64   Interestingly, I never knew anyone accuse the new authorities of bullying etc., only the old. Of course, there is more than one possible explanation for this. Perhaps the new authorities were much more sensitive or attuned to the sensibilities of their staff. It seems to me, however, that this was unlikely. New authorities, especially when composed of the formerly subordinate, are rarely gentle in exerting their authority over anyone. It seems to me much more likely that the complainants understood, with the cunning given to those who need to know on which side their bread is buttered, where power now lay, and furthermore that the new masters wanted them to complain against the old. This did not mean that they liked the new masters, on the contrary; in my experience, they had nothing but contempt for them.

65   On this subject, I recommend a brilliant and devastating account of the distortion by tort law of responses to accidents and other untoward events, entitled *Whiplash and Other Useful Illnesses*, by Dr Andrew Malleson, McGill Queens University Press, 2002. It is not only the legal system, but commercial insurers, who benefit from such distortions. For example, I once examined a claimant under an insurance policy who appeared to me to be making his symptoms up. I advised the insurance company that they needed a private detective more than a doctor. Somewhat to my surprise, the insurance company engaged a private detective, who filmed the claimant in activities completely incompatible with his previous claim: so incompatible, in fact, that his claim must have been consciously and deliberately fraudulent rather than merely mistaken or exaggerated. I asked the insurance company whether it intended to prosecute him, to which it replied that it never prosecuted such cases because it thought that to do so would give the company a bad name for harshness and lack of sympathy with its clients. This seemed to me a grotesquely sentimental notion (if it was actually held, which I doubted), for to allow such fraudulent claims to be put forward without

prosecution was actually to encourage them, and it was the honest clients' premiums that would rise as a result. Surely honest clients of the company — if there were any — would welcome prosecution of those who made fraudulent claims, which would help to contain the cost of their premiums? In fact, as I soon realised, the insurance company had no interest whatever in containing the cost of the clients' premiums: it would merely pass on the added cost of benefits paid out to fraudulent claimants with a surcharge for its own profit. The mystery of the case was that the insurance company employed a private detective in the first place, and subsequently refused to pay out the benefits. That the claimant was a true professional was illustrated by the fact that, though he knew himself to be a fraud, he launched an appeal against the company's decision. He knew that, under the rules of the insurance industry's association, benefits must be paid out, on a non-refundable basis, until the appeal is decided one way or another, and irrespective of its outcome. The fraudulent claimant knew that, bureaucracy being what it is, the appeal would not be decided for at least a year: and so he would receive benefits for that length of time, come what might. Thus two thoroughly sentimental notions, that no client of an insurance company should be prosecuted for a fraudulent claim, and that non-refundable benefits should be paid pending the result of an appeal, in effect defrauded policy-holders of their money. The insurance company was as dishonest as the fraudulent claimant. Only in a society in which self-attributed victimhood entitled a person to special consideration could such a thing be considered normal.

66 *More than Victims: Battered Women, the Syndrome Society and the Law*, Donald Alexander Downs, Chicago, 1996. In American trials of women who had killed their chronically abusive husbands, it was sometimes argued that the women were deprived of their normal legal responsibility not to kill because of psychological consequences of chronic abuse.

67   Likewise, no one is so much a determinist that he attributes his own good deeds to ineluctable causes apart, perhaps, from his own innate goodness. Only when he has done something bad does the determinist invoke such causes in his own case. It is astonishing how many such causes most of us can find within a few seconds of the commencement of the search.

68   A precondition for a new integration [of the personality] ' wrote Bettelheim, 'is acceptance of how severely one has been traumatized, and of what the nature of the trauma has been.' In other words, in order to root out mood swings, or the habit of shouting, screaming, and sobbing when one does not get one's own way, it is necessary to find the buried psychological treasure whose uncovery will in itself put an end to all unruliness and unhappiness. This means dwelling practically *ad infinitum* upon the unpleasant events in a person's life. There is, of course, never any shortage of material: for what person can have sojourned on earth for longer than a few years without having encountered much unpleasantness? When this fails to remove the propensity to mood swings, it is concluded that the mood-swinger has been dwelling on the wrong unpleasantnesses, the real ones responsible for their condition lying at even deeper levels of the psyche.

69   It is interesting that women who become prison visitors and fall in love with prisoners rarely do so with petty criminals. Shoplifters do not interest them, disqualified drivers who continue to drive hold no charms for them. On the contrary, they often go straight for the jugular, as it were: murder, the more brutal the better, and sometimes of a previous lover or spouse. The further a man has fallen, the greater his potential elevation, the more spectacular his redemption, by the love of the prison visitor. The elevation and redemption often do not last long: see *Dream Lovers* by Jacquelynne Wilcox-Bailey, Wakefield Press, for spectacular cases. Of course, it is always dangerous to speak of the denominator without knowing the numerator, on this occasion the number of prison visitors whose association with

murderers turns out well.

70 This is not mere ignorance of the meaning of those signs. When I asked a woman with an abusive sexual consort how long it would take me, if I met him, to guess that he was no good, there was a very high chance, probably of the order of eight out of ten, that they would reply that I would know immediately, as he came through the door. I pointed out that if she knew that I would know, she knew, at least implicitly, what it was about him that would tell me. This being the case, she had knowingly exposed herself to abuse, and therefore, while she was indeed his victim (and personally I advocated severe punishment of such men), she could not claim to be *just* his victim. She was in part the co-author of her own misery. And when I suggested that, if ever she consorted with another man, having thrown over her current abuser, she brought him to me for my inspection, so that I could tell her in advance whether she should go out with him or not, she invariably got the point and laughed.

71 For example, by the tattoos of the words LOVE and HATE on the knuckles of his hands. I wish I had the space to elaborate on the dermatological semiotics of violence in England.

72 I speak as one without any religious belief.

73 I do not mean to imply that there is no such thing as injustice; but it requires judgment as to when and where it exists. Suffering and unhappiness *ipso facto* cannot be evidence of it.

74 The sentimentality of Christianity is in supposing that a time will come when this will change.

75 The best euphemism that I have ever heard for murder is 'He was shown the red card.' The referee at a football match shows the red card when he sends a player off the field for very bad behaviour. 'He was shown the red card:' i.e. He was sent off the pitch of life.

76 The European Union is, of course, a means by which aging politicians can retain their importance for the rest of their lives without subjecting themselves to the humiliations, inconveniences

and tedium of elections.

77 In his diary entry for 28 July, 1986, the British aesthetic snob James Lees-Milne vented his irritation at the spectacle of pop stars holding concerts, under the rubric of Band Aid, to help the victims of a famine in Africa. He wrote: 'Band Aid, the crusade to help starving Africans who take everything and give nothing, and want weeding out, not encouraging to multiply.' This is authentically horrible, especially as it is obviously sincere and deeply-felt. What are starving people supposed to give in return for a little food, what actually can they give? Who exactly needs weeding out, and by what means? Lees-Milne appears completely oblivious to the ignoble and vicious consequences of the use of such metaphors applied to human populations. Just because Band Aid was an organisation of self-promoting sentimental hypocrites does not mean that famine in Africa is a good thing.

78 Doe was a member of the Krahn tribe, which was roughly 3 per cent of the population of Liberia: more or less the same proportion as that of the Americo-Liberians whose rule he overthrew in the name of equality under the law.

79 Like Mr Brown, he studied at Edinburgh University. The influence of Scotland and Scotsmen on African dictators would perhaps make an interesting monograph: Nyerere, Amin and, of course, His Excellency the Life President Ngwazi Dr H. Kamuzu Banda (even now I can hardly conceive of his as just Banda) spring to mind.

80 It was not, however, politically incompetent. An extremely poor country is one in which it is easy to confer economic privileges to a small political elite, which is then beholden to the leadership. In a sense, the worse the better — to quote Lenin. A man cannot be described as incompetent *tour court* who remains in power for more than a quarter of a century and dies in his bed.

81 In a chapbook in my possession, printed in Onitsha, Nigeria (the erstwhile centre of the Nigerian chapbook industry), the author states that you cannot get rich without making an effort.

The example he gives is that it is impossible to win a lottery without going to the effort of buying a ticket.

82 It is not only in Africa that this is a problem. The revolutionary guerrillas of Latin America were the product not of peasant desperation, but of the expansion of tertiary education beyond the capacity of the economy to absorb its products. The worst of all these guerrilla groups, Sendero Luminoso of Peru, that undoubtedly would have committed atrocities equal to those of Pol Pot and the Khmer Rouge had it not been defeated just in time, was actually started on the campus of Ayacucho University by a professor of philosophy who had written his thesis on Kant. In Britain, it is no accident, as the Marxists used to say, that bureaucracy has increased *pari passu* with the expansion of tertiary education, usually in subjects of no vocational and often scant intellectual value. Something has to be done with all the graduates if they are not to become professional malcontents. In her latest book, the crime writer P.D. James draws attention to the paradox, or absurdity, that the British government wants to send fifty per cent of the school-leaving population to university while forty per cent of the same population can barely read. Of course, lengthening educational careers, and making people pay for it, is a way of getting young people to fund their own unemployment.

83 Smith starts his book with the following paragraph: How selfish soever man may be supposed, there are evidently some principles in his nature, which interest him in the fortune of others, and render their happiness necessary to him, though he derives nothing from it except the pleasure of seeing it. Of this kind is pity or compassion, the emotion which we feel for the misery of others, when we either see it, or are made to conceive it in a very lively manner. That we often derive sorrow from the sorrow of others, is a matter of fact too obvious to require any instances to prove it; for this sentiment, like all the other original passions of human nature, is by no means confined to the virtuous and humane, though they perhaps may feel it with the

most exquisite sensibility. The greatest ruffian, the most hardened violator of the laws of society, is not altogether without it.

[84] It is true that you can be morally responsible for bringing about an irreparable situation. But that is another question.

[85] In contrast, say, to an assessment of the effects of the Nazi occupation of Poland, where the precise quantum of damage may perhaps be disputed, but not the fact of colossal and overwhelming damage.

[86] Goering was, in fact, a great anti-vivisectionist, and there exists a cartoon of all the liberated laboratory animals giving him the Nazi salute.

[87] Though it is not all that difficult. A lot of the money will be wasted. Oxfam Trading — that runs charity shops in Great Britain — manages to extract 17 per cent profit on turnover, despite the fact that its shops have favourable local tax rates, most of the staff are unpaid volunteers, and all its goods for sale cost it nothing. A second-hand bookseller pointed out to me what a disgrace this was. He made as much profit on turnover, despite having to pay for his stock and having no preferential tax rates. A person wanting to make a donation to charity by means of books would be better off selling his books to a commercial second-hand seller and giving the money he received — between a third and a half of the eventual sale price — away directly. To give goods to Oxfam is therefore primarily to support the professionals who run it. Incidentally, it is worth pointing out also that the government in Britain, being by far the largest contributor to most important charities, has turned them into appendages of the state. Charity in Britain has become a surreptitious form of taxation.

[88] Somalis as individuals are another thing entirely. I am a great admirer of the redoubtable Ayan Hirsi Ali, for example, who is surely one of the bravest people on the planet, but is completely without exhibitionism. She cares about truth and she cares about freedom. There are fewer such people than might be supposed,

or hoped for. It is perfectly possible that there are many other Somalis of her ilk.

[89] It may even have played a part in the genesis of the credit crisis of 2007-08. The Community Investment Act of 1977, as enforced under the presidency of William Clinton, required banks to lend money for mortgages to people not on the basis of their creditworthiness, but on the basis of their ethnicity and residence of relatively impoverished neighbourhoods. Before that requirement, defaults on mortgages ran at the same rate between all ethnic groups i.e. the banks were lending to people of all ethnicities according to objective standards of creditworthiness. Easy credit led, not surprising, to easy default. A gimcrack sentimental idea was forced upon banks. I am not sufficiently expert in the field, however, to know what proportion of the responsibility for the credit crisis is borne by it.

Index